D1217380

Toward an Open Tomb

TOWARD AN OPEN TOMB

The Crisis of Israeli Society

by MICHEL WARSCHAWSKI

Translated by PETER DRUCKER

MONTHLY REVIEW PRESS

New York

Library of Congress Cataloging-in-Publication Data

Warschawski, Michel.
   [Tombeau ouvert. English]
   The crisis of Israeli society / by Michel Warschawski ;
translated by Peter Drucker.
      p. cm.
   Includes index.
      ISBN 1-58367-109-9 (pbk.) — ISBN 1-58367-110-2 (cloth)
1. Palestinian Arabs—Government policy—Israel. 2. Israel—Politics and
government—1993- 3. Arab-Israeli conflict—1993- I. Title.
   JC574.2.U6A46 2004
   320.51'0973—DC22

                        2004009353

MONTHLY REVIEW PRESS
122 West 27th Street
New York, NY 10001
www.monthlyreview.org

Printed in Canada

10 9 8 7 6 5 4 3 2 1

Contents

To the memory of my comrades Yankel Taut (Misha) and Ruth (Trude)
Milo, anti-Nazi fighters in Germany and anticolonialist fighters
in Palestine-Israel, who died in 2002 after seventy years of struggle.

I never go to the movies unless I'm promised that the film will have a happy ending. I really don't like stories that turn out badly. It's not much of a surprise, then, that I have had a lot of trouble writing this essay, which attempts to chart Israel's mad course toward its own destruction. With each chapter, each paragraph, and each example that shows the horror of today's reality, I often wrote with tears in my eyes. Sometimes these were tears of rage at the boundless violence of the repression and the dehumanization of other human beings. But sometimes they were tears of sorrow at the degeneration of a society that is my society, too, in which my grandchildren are going to grow up.

Obviously, I would have preferred to talk about the light at the end of the tunnel, and give people new hope by describing the forms of resistance that still do exist in Israel. Mustn't we do everything possible not to "let the bastards get you down"? But besides the fact that I've just devoted another book to dissident voices in Israel, I think it's dishonest to try always to give a balanced picture; always to repeat the refrain that we sang in the Boy Scouts, that "every cloud has a silver lining." We've all seen dark, menacing clouds with no silver lining whatsoever.

There are some stories that turn out badly, dreams that descend into nightmares, and adventures that end in catastrophe. Zionism could well turn out to be a passing episode in Jewish history, a parenthesis that has been both brutal (for its victims) and tragic (for its protagonists). The second kingdom of Israel was shorter and less glorious than the first; why can't the third be even more ephemeral and even less honorable?

In *On the Border*, I posed the question of whether there is a point of no return.[1] When do you know that a battle has definitely been lost, that the bad guys have won this round and that our children's or grandchildren's generation will have to take on the work of rebuilding? I have kept on asking this same question of my revolutionary comrades who had fled from the Nazis and immediately taken up the battle under skies that were sunnier but not much more clement. They have never been able to give me an answer. But their lives, their choices, and their struggles have provided me nonetheless with a political and moral compass, an example for me to follow, particularly in those moments when it seems to be midnight in our century.

My comrades Yankel Taut (Misha) and Ruth (Trude) Milo, German revolutionary socialists, internationalist and anti-Stalinist militants, who taught my comrades as well as me that when our societies are riding "full tilt over a cliff" toward barbarism, we owe it to ourselves to chart our steps with optimism of the will, despite the pessimism that our intellects impose on us. And if despite everything the intellect wins out over the will, there still remains one last logic of the struggle against injustice: resistance. It is simply the outraged cry of human dignity, and the refusal to surrender to brute force.

PREAMBLE: BEACH STORIES

July 2002, on the Tel Aviv beach: in two hours a concert will begin in the docks of the old port in solidarity with reservists resisting military service, organized by the movement Yesh Gvul. The big names of Israeli rock music had agreed to play at the concert free in order to express their opposition to the policy of repression in the occupied territories. We've just heard that most of them have backed out at the last minute, under pressure from threats of being boycotted by the radio networks and some of their sponsors.

With a French friend who has the peculiar habit of spending her vacations in Israel, we're about to go to one of the beach kiosks for a drink. Suddenly there's a terrible racket: more than a hundred yards away, in the courtyard of a disco, a team of technicians is doing sound checks. We can't hear each other, and the checks drag on for long minutes. My friend decides to ask them to lower the volume.

Speaking a very correct Hebrew, though with a strong French accent and a very un-Israeli smile and courtesy, she explains that the noise is infernal and is bothering many people who came to the beach for some peace and quiet. The answer: "Get lost, you fuckin' whore. Jeez, who do you think you are? Go back to your own country with all the other anti-Semites. If you want to do charity work, go join the Red Cross. Get out of here before I smash your face in." Yet the technician doesn't look like a lowlife. He looks more like someone from a good family, as the saying goes.

Dumbfounded by the technician's rudeness, with tears in her eyes, my friend moves away toward the old port in silence. Then after a long pause, she says, "I can't stand this constant tension. This isn't the first time something like this has happened to me. I'm afraid for Israel. They've blown their tops. In the thirty years I've been coming here, I've never seen such violence in daily life. Your society is sick, terribly sick."

August 2002, on a beach near Haifa: Pnina and her friends are in the sun getting a tan. Just in front of them a father is playing racket-ball with his son. Right next to them is a big sign that says playing ball games is forbidden here. Pnina remarks that there's an area specially reserved for games less than ten yards away, but where they are, games are forbidden. The father starts yelling that if they don't like what he's doing they can move, the beach belongs to everyone, etc. The friends respond gently but firmly that they're only asking him to respect the rules of the beach. Apparently losing interest in his game, he leaves with his son. But after a few steps he turns back and asks Pnina and her friends, in a mixture of anger and resentment, "But why should I be the only one in this country who obeys the laws?"

When I heard this story, I decided to write this book.

1. Green Light for a Massacre

For more than three decades the Israeli army has used an oxymoron to describe its activities in the Palestinian territories that have been under its authority since June 1967: "the liberal occupation." This semantic device resembles other oxymorons of the same type, like the "purity of our weapons" and the "Jewish and democratic state."[1]

Two important elements are behind this notion of a "liberal occupation," however. On the one hand Israel wants to show a liberal face to the world (in the US sense of the term), not a brutal, colonialist face. On the other hand, Israel had the declared intention of carrying out an occupation policy with a minimum of repressive measures and a minimal number of victims among the population.

Admittedly, the liberal face did not make it through the first intifada; 1,500-odd Palestinian victims in less than three years demonstrated that an occupation was bloody and repressive by definition, especially if the people under occupation massively manifested their desire for freedom and independence. It was precisely the fact that the occupation could no longer claim to be liberal that led to a shift in public opinion toward withdrawal from the occupied territories and, two years later, to massive support for the Oslo process.

Since September 2000, the Israeli occupation has stopped pretending to be liberal. On the contrary, it is openly displaying its "brilliant, cruel" character, to borrow the words of the Irgun anthem. (The Irgun was the ancestor of the Likud Party now in power.) The occupation is brutal and bloody—and the great majority of the Israeli public backs it.

As early as September 2000 the Israeli government gave the order to carry out the plan for across-the-board repression prepared two years earlier by a man who later became commanding general of the Israeli army. One chapter of the plan is called "Bloodbath."[2] This was one of the scenarios that the high command proposed to Ehud Barak as a possible response to a unilateral Palestinian declaration of independence. The common denominator of all these scenarios was to make sure that Palestinians paid through the nose for their insubordination, and for the uppityness that a unilateral initiative on their part would have shown.

The unilateral initiative in September 2000 was the start of the second intifada, a popular revolt—an unarmed popular revolt in its first weeks—against the Israeli occupation. We cannot emphasize the fact enough: Palestinian soldiers joined in the confrontations with the Israeli army only *after* Israeli soldiers armed to the teeth, often with rifles with telescopic lenses, had killed several dozen young demonstrators. As for the bombings in Israel, these only began three months later, by which time several hundred Palestinians had died.

The Israeli orders are clear: break any form of resistance, by any means. The target hardly matters, the circumstances hardly matter, and the extent of "collateral damage" hardly matters.

To begin with, in keeping with the scenario mentioned early, the Israeli repression had an essentially punitive character. It was meant to teach the Palestinians a lesson for having dared to defy the occupation, and above all for having dared to reject Ehud Barak's "extremely generous offer" at Camp David—-which we will come back to. At this stage it is important to understand that the goal Barak and the high command had set was not "restoring order" but carrying out a punitive campaign, which would quickly be transformed into a campaign of pacification.

A campaign of this kind involves massive use of military means to terrorize a civilian population, in order to force it to accept colonial rule and the forms of domination that the rulers seek to impose. In order to justify violence against civilians in the eyes of domestic and international public opinion, the population must be stripped of its civilian status at whatever cost. This accounts for the systematic use of the concept of terrorism, in the occupied Palestinian territories as in Chechnya: in this way bloody repression of a civilian population can be disguised as a "war on terrorism." The people the fragmentation bombs are tearing apart are no longer women and children; it is no longer entire families that the state of siege is reducing to poverty and sometimes to hunger; they are all "terrorists." The concept of "war" is also important in its own way. It gives the impression that the world's fifth-strongest military power is facing not a civilian population but a rival military force, thus justifying the use of armored cars, combat helicopters, and fighter planes.

September 11, 2001, clearly enabled the Israeli authorities to extend their use of the concept "war on terrorism." It gave new legitimacy to the most brutal methods of repression. In fact the attack on the Twin Towers gave the US administration an opportunity to create a new, planetary, juridical and political code in which the war on terrorism justifies pretty much anything: from bombing civilian populations in order to flush terrorists into the open to preventive war, by way of suspending constitutional and human rights—as the horrors of Camp Guantánamo show.

FROM MUHAMMAD EL-DURA TO THE DESTRUCTION OF RAMALLAH

The violence of the new wave of repression in the occupied territories was visible from the first day, with the killing of young Muhammad el-Dura in his father's arms near the Netsarim settlement in the Gaza Strip. According to the Israeli army's own rules—at least, the rules that had been in force before the second intifada—Muhammad el-Dura had been murdered in cold blood. As long as he was not endangering any soldier, shooting at him was forbidden—all the more so if he was a child, all the more so if he was unarmed.

Only a year after the events did Israeli army spokespeople decide to deny everything wholesale. More than a year went by before anyone dared to assert that the child's own father had deliberately brought about his death—from Palestinian bullets. (Note that this tactic of blaming the victim was received with less credulity in Israel than in certain milieus abroad.)

During the first week of clashes, the impressive number of Palestinian victims, many of them young or very young, in most cases killed by bullets fired from such a distance that the Israeli soldiers could not have been in danger, showed that the soldiers had orders to shoot to kill. This meant a break with earlier instructions, which authorized soldiers to shoot only if they were being fired on or if they were in danger. According to a report by the Israeli human rights organization B'tselem:

> When the intifada began, the IDF... expanded the range of situations in which soldiers are permitted to open fire.... The new version of the Open-Fire Regulations, which according to press reports are referred to as "Blue Lilac," have remained secret.

But they were prepared several months before this intifada broke out.[3] Again: during the course of this first week use of firearms by Palestinians was still rare; the Israeli soldiers were up against teenagers, armed at most with slingshots.

This sharp shift in Israeli behavior is a central element in the strategy that the high command had been planning for a long time; its primary goal is to punish the Palestinians for daring to defy the occupation. Whatever progress is made or setbacks encountered in the negotiations under way, Israel will not tolerate any initiative, diplomatic or popular, that the Jewish state has not previously discussed and ratified.

The harshness of the measures that the occupation authorities took from the first days of the clashes is directly proportional to the double humiliation that the government and public opinion felt: at the rejection of Barak's "generous offer," and at the challenge to the Pax Israeliana that the majority of Israelis had also been generous enough to grant.

It nonetheless became clear quite soon that young Palestinians were refusing to learn the lesson that the Israeli soldiers were trying to drill into their thick skulls with live ammunition. The oldest among them, enraged at seeing their unarmed brothers and children mowed down, decided to take advantage of the rudimentary weapons that the Oslo accords had allowed them to acquire. This is of course the most natural reaction for anyone who has a weapon and sees his neighbor being shot at without being able to defend himself. But it is also a trap. It made it possible from then on to present the teenagers' popular, unarmed revolt as an armed struggle, a life-and-death struggle, a war—and in war, all is fair.

The escalation took place rapidly. On November 9, 2000, the policy of "extrajudicial executions" began with the assassination of Hussein Abayat. Between November 2000 and the end of August 2001, according to Amnesty International, at least fifty Palestinians fell victim to this kind of assassination.[4] "Active defense" and "preventive self-defense" are the terms that the Israeli cabinet uses to refer to acts defined in international law as war crimes. The "collateral damage" associated with these attacks amounts to over 65 percent (again as per Amnesty International): with thirty activists targeted, at least twenty non-targeted people were killed.[5] Virtually no protest came from political leaders or intellectuals, nor did the courts make any objection. The Labor-Meretz government, the same one that made the "generous offer," adopted this policy of assassinations in the framework of "Israel's battle to survive."

At the same time Israel began using Apache helicopters to fire missiles at buildings located in residential areas. On July 31, 2001, eight people, including two children, were killed when two missiles were fired at the offices of the Palestinian Information Center in Nablus. After the helicopters, F-16 fighter planes were deployed; then when the self-governing towns were invaded in February 2002, armored car units were massively employed.

Bombers and armored cars are not the means traditionally used to dismantle terrorist networks; and in fact are ineffective for this purpose. They are used to wage war on enemy army units. Clearly no such units existed on the Palestinian side. The "war" has thus in reality been a war on civilians, their homes, their infrastructure and their institutions.

The Israeli offensive in the occupied territories showed its true face during the attack on Palestinian towns in the winter of 2002. The army's destructive rage took on previously unheard-of dimensions. More than ten infantry regiments and armored cars carried out savage attacks on public and private buildings, telephone poles and lines, sidewalks and shoulders of the streets.

Two days after the Israeli army's withdrawal from Ramallah in March 2002, I got past the blockades in order to see the effects of the offensive with my own eyes. It was as if the city had been wiped out by a natural disaster. Nothing had been spared, not even the few children's playgrounds. Missiles and shells had been used to demolish the buildings that housed Palestinian Authority agencies, military and civilian: the ministry of education, the ministry of culture, the statistical bureau, etc. The soldiers, not satisfied with destroying official Palestinian Authority institutions, had fired shells at schools and even at several clinics. I saw that the Sakakini Cultural and Artistic Center had been sacked and some of its works of art deliberately destroyed.

But what illustrated the Israeli army's vandalism in Ramallah (as in other West Bank cities) more than anything else was the trashing of private apartments, the systematic destruction of sidewalks, and the hundreds of cars crushed by tanks.[6] None of this had anything to do with security or with fighting terrorism—unless you consider the entire Palestinian people a terrorist people. This is what it was all about. As early as October 2000, and still more after Ariel Sharon's victory in February 2001, Palestinian society as a whole became the enemy, the object that had to be eradicated—"like a cancer," as commanding general Moshe Yaalon said later. Even if the destructive rage was not functional from a strict security standpoint, neither was it irrational. It was an integral part of an overall plan that aimed to crush the Palestinian population of the West Bank and Gaza, so as to force the Palestinians to surrender and accept Israel's "solutions."

. . . TO THE JENIN MASSACRE

Unspeakable horror.[7] Scraps of earlier lives. Endless debris forms a tragic landscape, a moonscape; we're on another planet. We'll need more time to understand the reality that this bare surface is covering: a boundless sorrow. Collective, personal mourning for all the people we've met. Everyone has lost friends and family; people show us orphaned children taken in by uncles or aunts. This one has lost a brother, a sister, a mother, a husband; this one's house was leveled; this one's husband, brother or son is a prisoner—somewhere far away; there's no news of him. All people know is where the camps are, near Ramallah, or near Gaza, in the desert.

We keep on being surprised by the scale and rage of this violence, which for twelve days struck and smashed and ravaged and demolished and killed and destroyed and carried off this camp, whose inhabitants were shut up in it as if it were a mousetrap. Enough to drive you mad.

What you mistake at first for aloofness or distance is the stunned condition of people who are literally "groggy" from a cataclysm of violence, whose trail of destruction is all we can see. This is the comparison that often comes to mind: these people have just been through a natural disaster: an earthquake or a tidal wave.[8]

Why Jenin? What made this little town in the northern West Bank, or strictly speaking the refugee camp next door to it, the symbol of the horror and violence of Israeli repression in the occupied territories? Why Jenin rather than the Balata camp in Nablus or Khan Yunis in the Gaza Strip, where the army also resorted to wholesale destruction and killing of civilians? Why do people talk about the "massacre" in Jenin but not elsewhere? Why did the UN Security Council decide to set up a commission of inquiry on the Jenin massacre but not on the dozens of targeted assassinations or the murder by elite marksmen of dozens of Palestinians less than sixteen years old?

The primary reason is that there *was* a massacre in Jenin, that is, systematic killing of civilians, either by shooting them in the head or by burying them alive under the wreckage of their houses. Crimes like this took place as well during the invasion of Palestinian towns three months earlier; but then these were still the exception. In Jenin, too, many civilians were killed, their deaths to be seen simply as "collateral damage" of the policy of destruction—which, by the way, was far more horrible in Jenin than what took place in the earlier invasion of towns.

In its report on the Jenin camp Human Rights Watch describes, on the basis of specific eyewitness testimony, twenty-two cases of assassinations and "illegal executions."[9] I limit myself here to mentioning four:

Murder of Abdel Karim el-Sadi and Wadh Shalabi, as recounted by the correspondent of the London *Independent*:

> Fathi Shalabi watched his son die. The two men were standing side by side with their hands up when Israeli soldiers opened fire on them. Mr Shalabi's son, Wadh, and another man who was with them died instantly, but the 63-year-old Mr Shalabi survived. He lay on the ground pretending to be dead for more than an hour while his son's blood gathered around him....
>
> Mr Shalabi described what took place. Soldiers ordered his family and Mr Al-Sadi down a narrow alley. "In cover behind the corner were four

soldiers. The two young men with me were carrying baby children, and the soldiers did not shoot at them."

Wadh Shalabi was carrying his four-month-old son, Mahmoud. The soldiers ordered the men to hand the children over to their mothers and told the women and children to go into the next-door house....

"The soldiers were about three metres away. I heard the names of two of them; they were Gaby and David. ... Suddenly Gaby shouted 'Kill them, kill them!'"[10]

Kamal Zghair, invalid, murdered in his wheelchair. Durar Hussein tells the story:

> That morning he came to see me as usual. I washed his clothes and put them out to dry. About 4 in the afternoon, I pushed his wheelchair up to the street. He went on on his own toward the gas station. I had attached a white flag to his wheelchair to be sure that they could see it from a distance. I waited about ten minutes, because it takes time to get to the edge of the lot.
>
> I heard tanks coming from the west. I started to worry about him in the street. Just at that moment they started firing from the tanks. I knew exactly where he was, and that's where the shots were coming from. At first I thought they were warning shots. The tanks were getting closer and it was getting too dangerous to stay outside, so I went back in....
>
> [The next morning] I went out on foot. I saw the wheelchair, but I didn't see him. I ran to the gas station where he slept, I went into his room, but no one was there. I went back to the place where I'd found his wheelchair and looked everywhere. I found his body in the grass. He was unrecognizable; his face and legs had been completely crushed. I knew it was him because he was wearing the shoes that I'd washed the night before.

Jamal Fayid, buried alive by a bulldozer. His sister tells the story:

We begged the soldiers; we told them there was a disabled person in the house. We even showed them his identity card. The ones in the street told us to go away. So we went to see other soldiers in another house and told them the same thing. We begged and begged. Finally they let five women into the house to try to get him out.

Fayid's mother, sister and aunt and two neighbors went into the house. From inside the house they heard a bulldozer coming.

It got there and started to demolish the house. We heard people outside shouting, "Stop! There are women in there! Stop!" The soldiers knew perfectly well that we were in there because they'd given us permission themselves to go in to look for Jamal.

Despite the shouts, the bulldozer kept going. The women left the house, which was collapsing around them, burying the paralyzed Fayid in the wreckage. The soldier in the bulldozer insulted them and called them whores. The military doctor who had helped them the night before was angry and yelled at the driver of the bulldozer.

Afaf Disuki, torn to ribbons by a bomb while soldiers laughed. His thirty-seven-year-old sister Aisha Disuki tells the story:

We were inside and saw the smoke. The soldiers asked us to open the door. My sister went to open the door, and at that moment the grenade exploded. So we all started shouting to call an ambulance. The soldiers just laughed. We saw that the whole right side of Afaf's face was torn off and his shoulder and left arm were wounded.

Ashaman Abu Murad, who was outside with the soldiers, confirms that they were laughing: "After the explosion I heard his sisters shouting and calling for an ambulance. The soldiers were laughing."

The exact number of victims will never be known. The Israeli army buried some of the bodies; the international commission of inquiry, mandated among other things to confirm or refute the charge that there was a massacre, was kept from carrying out its mission. But in a sense the number of victims is not the most important thing. Most important is the unrestrained violence that accompanied Operation Defensive Shield and, more specifically, the conquest of the Jenin refugee camp. The reason the army initially overestimated the number of Palestinian victims,[11] as we will see, is precisely that it was aware of this murderous rage, which took no account of the fact that civilians were facing tanks and missiles. The army knew perfectly well that its soldiers had killed unarmed people in cold blood.

The camp's residents, though used to the violence of the Israeli occupation, felt right away that this total lack of restraint, this boundless brutality, was different. Barely a few hours after the Israeli armored cars entered the camp, Leila Shahid, who was stationed in Palestine at the time, was phoning solidarity movements in France in tears and begging them, "Do something! What's happening in the Jenin camp is a real massacre."

Between the occupation of Ramallah and the Jenin camp massacre, another two months had gone by. While there is continuity in the operations of Israel's occupying army, there are also escalations. Each operation has the goal of testing the reactions—from both Israeli public opinion and the international community—and if the criticisms are not too serious, establishing a new standard level of violence. As I write these lines in September 2002, the standard level established by Operation Defensive Shield has not yet been surpassed. The plans for "transfer," that is a vast ethnic cleansing operation on the West Bank, will doubtless be the next leap forward in the level of horror, if the war U.S. against Iraq provides an opportunity for this.

ON THE MISUSE OF "SELF-DEFENSE"

Israeli repression in the occupied territories is justified—by those who organize it as well as by public opinion—in the name of "self-defense." This is at the least an unwarranted use of the term. When the Israeli cabinet defined extrajudicial executions on July 4, 2001, as a policy of "active defense," and later (on October 3) as "preventive self-defense," it was using Orwellian rhetorical strategies. This invidious definition of self-defense must be linked not only to the Israeli authorities' deliberate decision to present colonial repression in the occupied territories as "a war," but also to a very specific conception of war. In this conception of war the individual, civilian or military, is stripped of all rights, including the right to stay alive.

As early as October 2001, the army characterized the new situation in the occupied territories as an "armed conflict that is not yet a full-fledged war." "Not yet" and "full-fledged" do not figure in politicians' speeches or the orders given to military units, of course. But these reservations are important for the authorities, because they are supposed to exempt them from the obligations imposed in wartime under international conventions and the customary law of war.

In January 2001 Ehud Barak, at the time prime minister and minister of defense, justified the extrajudicial executions in a letter to the Israeli High Court:

> International law authorizes strikes at individuals when it has been established beyond a doubt that they are preparing to commit attacks on Israeli targets.... This is a consequence, in a general sense, of a wartime situation, and more specifically of the right of self-defense.

Besides the fact that international law explicitly forbids executions of civilians or prisoners of war, there are two aspects of the prime minister's argument that need emphasizing, because they provide an ideological framework — and even a mental framework — for erasing any limits on the conduct of the Israeli armed forces, and therefore for erasing any limits on the systematic policy of murders and massacres.[12] Consider first the flexible use of tenses: what does "are preparing to" mean? Is there evidence of a concrete, immediate danger? In the great majority of cases, the answer is no. According to the intelligence services, the person designated for execution intends to commit "attacks on Israeli targets." We should note that it is legitimate in wartime to "attack Israeli targets"; intentions of this kind have never made it permissible for an army to liquidate generals "because they intended to attack" enemy targets. Then, as a logical consequence, there is a semantic slippage from concrete acts to an overall political project: every Palestinian, or at least every Palestinian patriot, is perceived in the new Israeli discourse as having decide to challenge, if not Israel's very existence, then at least the form and frontiers that the Jewish state's leaders choose to give it. He or she thus becomes an active element in a project for destroying Israeli national existence. Neutralizing him or her is thus an imperative of self-defense.

This leads to the central notion of preventive security, and to an extremely broad definition of it. It is necessary not just to prevent specific attacks, but also to defeat a general, structured will to destroy the state of Israel. The targets are no longer specific militants involved in concrete acts and posing a threat to specific individuals, but rather Palestinians in general, involved in a national liberation struggle.

In conclusion, understanding Israeli strategy in the occupied territories requires remembering that the strategy was elaborated and set in motion several months *before* the first wave of suicide bombings, at a time when the Palestinians were carrying on an essentially civilian struggle limited to the occupied territories. Only later did the conflict spill over into Israeli territory and did the suicide bombings begin again, after a very long period in which they had been stopped.

2. A Double Dehumanization

In 2000, most Israelis were hungry for peace, or at least for normality. Despite a certain skepticism that had taken root in public opinion following the bombings (which were themselves a response to systematic violations of the agreements signed by successive Israeli governments, and to the Palestinians' growing humiliation in the occupied territories), the Israeli people did not want to go back to the pre-Oslo situation. To break the Oslo process, it was indispensable to convince public opinion that it had been a trap—a trap all the more dangerous because it was hidden behind the rhetoric of peace and reconciliation. This was the mystification that Barak pulled off after Camp David. (I will come back to this.)

What has to be understood as we analyze the radical change in Israeli treatment of the Palestinians is that in order to neutralize the widespread desire for peace and tranquility, an existential, global danger had to be conjured up. Terrorist networks were far from frightening enough to do the trick. It was absolutely necessary to demonize the whole Palestinian people. The message had to be: we are preventing a second Holocaust by repressing a terrorist people that want to drive the Jews into the sea.

Only this way of arguing makes it possible to understand how Israel can talk about "self-defense" and "preventive repression," when Israeli military, economic, and even diplomatic superiority is overwhelming. Declaring that an entire people is an enemy and defining them as a terrorist organization necessarily leads to dehu-

manizing them. Israeli soldiers are no longer facing civilians but terrorists carrying out a plan for genocide.

The uprooting of whole orchards, massive destruction of houses and sometimes of whole neighborhoods, as in Rafah in the Gaza
Strip or the Jenin refugee camp, has been discussed at great length.
The argument used to justify these barbarous measures is the safety
of soldiers and settlers. The law of war recognizes this argument,
but with limits: it is linked to the principle of proportionality.
Bombing a whole village to wipe out a nest of sharpshooters is considered a war crime. Bombing a house in the middle of a residential
neighborhood with a one-ton bomb in order to liquidate an alleged
terrorist is considered a war crime. In these cases the "collateral
damage" is out of proportion to the objective.

In the occupied territories the principle of proportionality was
totally abandoned well before the start of the second intifada. Here
are two examples. Since 1995, the roughly 90,000 inhabitants of
the city of Bethlehem have been regularly forbidden from using
their main street; this is supposedly to ensure the safety of several
dozen observant Jews who sometimes come to pray at Rachel's
tomb in downtown Bethlehem. In Hebron the safety of the 150 settlers planted in the heart of downtown has required closing off
Martyrs Street and the produce market. Moreover, on every Jewish
holiday, at every moment of tension (stirred up in the great majority of cases by the settlers themselves), more than 100,000 Palestinian residents are placed under curfew, sometimes for weeks on
end. For years entire rows of fruit trees have been uprooted "to
ensure the settlers' safety"; for the last four years, for the same reason, whole hamlets have been displaced. Now whole villages are
being threatened with the same fate.

In the process of Israeli settlement, Palestinians are demoted
from the status of community to that of environmental problem,
which has to be moved or cleaned up as the needs of the occupation army or the whirlwind settlement program require. Since the

second intifada began and the myth of a life-and-death war was launched, this tendency has become much worse.

Since the beginning of 2001 the entire Palestinian population has been shut up in zones and micro-zones, without being able to move normally from one zone to the next. The lockdown instituted at the start of the "peace process" has been transformed into an encirclement of about a hundred towns and villages.[1] For the last three years, except for the collective taxis that shuttle back and forth between the various zones and the ambulances—if they are not blocked at the checkpoints—there are almost no Palestinian cars to be seen on West Bank roads. Agricultural products can seldom get out of the villages; industrial products can seldom get in. Economic life has been totally disrupted, as has family life and in fact normal social relations in general. For schoolchildren in the villages getting to school is a daily adventure. For sick people a hospital is an objective they can reach only after preparing a painstaking itinerary bypassing the checkpoints and linking up as many as five collective taxis and several miles on foot through the fields—with a chance of about 50 percent in the end of actually getting there. As for leaving the country, only a few privileged people have the right to do so.

A population of almost four million people has been literally imprisoned in order to ensure Israelis' safety, and above all in order to force them to capitulate and accept Barak's or Sharon's "generous offers." Passes are given out stingily, without taking medical, social, family, school or professional problems into account. For the military authorities there are no sick people, no students, no dying grandmother, only a terrorist population that has to be thwarted or forced to leave.

Even worse, precisely the signs of what the military sees as culture and civilization are the things that provoke them to the most destructive rage. There is no other way to explain the Israeli army's persistent hostility to computers. During the first invasion of Ramallah, the soldiers gathered all the computers in one of the ministries into one room and destroyed them all with a hand grenade or some other kind of explosive. Dehumanizing enemies requires eradicating anything that would tend to suggest that they are really civilized human beings.

This is also the profound reason for the military's persistent targeting of ambulances, hospitals and medical personnel, which was a great shock for a while to international public opinion. In March 2002 the Israeli human rights organization B'tselem published a report on Israeli occupation forces attacks on Palestinian medical personnel during the offensive against the Palestinian towns.[2] During the two first weeks of March, according to this report, soldiers attacked several dozen ambulances, leaving five dead among the medical personnel, including two doctors, and more than thirty wounded. The attacks were so systematic that the head of the International Red Cross mission, René Kousirnik, decided to publish a statement—something his organization almost never does—denouncing, in very undiplomatic language, the Israeli army's firing on Red Crescent ambulances. The ambulances were clearly marked with the Red Crescent logo, Kousirnik said, and their movements had been coordinated with the army. Speaking to a delegation from the Foreign Affairs Committee of the French Senate, the International Red Cross representative said, "The Israeli army grossly and deliberately violated the rules of the Geneva Convention…. I am shocked; nothing can justify this conduct."[3]

During Operation Defensive Shield, one month later, attacks on hospitals and medical personnel became still more common. If there were fewer victims among nurses, doctors, and ambulance staff, this was only because they were almost completely prevented from leaving the areas that the curfew confined them to. Those who defied orders in order to treat the wounded sometimes paid with their lives. In general, they were only able to observe from a distance the suffering of the wounded as they were losing blood, as the following example drawn from a Human Rights Watch report illustrates.

Hisham Samara, a hospital cook in Jenin, went with two nurses to a mosque where they heard people calling for help. A tank was stationed in the street.

> We took one of the nurse's scarves and made a white flag. I wound the white flag on a stick. I opened the door, and put my arm with the stick and the scarf outside of the mosque door. While I had my arm out, there was the sound of a big explosion.... Of course we tried to speak with the wounded man during all of this and try to get him to crawl towards us.... Both his hands were broken, he couldn't move them.

The medical personnel tried at least three times in the course of an hour and a half or two hours to get help for al-Haj, who was gradually losing blood. Two doctors in white coats, carrying white flags, tried to leave the mosque. They were forced back by a new explosion. Their efforts were hopeless. According to Samara the soldiers fired at al-Haj from the tank: "The tank fired at him and the bullets entered his back. It was a spray of fire, but it was not heavy tank fire." [4]

For the Israeli army there are no wounded people, only terrorists; there are no doctors, only terrorists in disguise; there are no ambulances, only cars camouflaged as ambulances carrying terrorists and explosives. [5]

Using Palestinians as human shields is another example of dehumanizing the adversary. This is one example from Operation Defensive Shield, picked out from dozens:

> Kamal Tawalbi, a forty-three-year-old father of fourteen children, and his fourteen-year-old son were also taken to the same house and forced to stand facing the Palestinian gunfire. The IDF soldiers also placed them at the windows and forced them to stand in front of the soldiers as the soldiers shot at Palestinian gunmen in the camp: "They put me in one corner and [my son] in the other corner [of the balcony]. The soldier put his gun on my shoulder. I was facing the soldier, we were face to face, with my back to the street. Then he started shooting. This situation lasted for three

hours. My son was in the same position—he was facing the soldier, the soldier had his gun on his shoulder, and was shooting." [6]

All these examples—of attacks on medical personnel, refusing medical help to the wounded, women in labor losing their babies
because they are not allowed to pass checkpoints, use of civilians as
human shields—show how little the occupation army bothers
about the lives of Palestinian men, women, or children. Security
requirements are always invoked to justify these crimes. But when
you give yourself the right in the name of security to deny the
adversary's humanity, the process of dehumanization cannot be
stopped. It simply becomes the way you always treat the "other
side," even when security no longer has anything to do with it.

The members of the ninth French civilian mission to Palestine
in February 2002 had the opportunity to experience this treatment
for themselves at a checkpoint in the Gaza Strip. They heard a
voice coming from a loudspeaker perched on top of a tower, shouting in Hebrew: "Men to the right, women to the left, five by five, on
your knees!" Only after crawling on their knees could Palestinians
pass the checkpoint. The media is full of examples of gratuitous
humiliations that have nothing to do with security: forcing men and
women to crawl on their knees, run naked or roll in the mud, for
example, or putting marks on their arms. For months now this has
no longer been a matter of a few isolated incidents or a few sadistic
soldiers, but a generalized pattern of behavior.

To finish off this quick sketch of the dehumanization of the
Palestinians, we need only visit Telmond prison, where more than
200 Palestinian minors are confined for fighting against the occupation. With reference to Palestinians, "minor" means under 16 years
old. Unlike young Jews in detention centers, these Palestinian children not only have no right to education, to listen to the radio or to
phone calls with their families; as a matter of course they may not
receive any visits from their parents. Their parents are denied the

necessary permits to enter Israeli territory, where the Telmond prison is.[7] For months at a time fourteen- and fifteen-year-old children are not allowed to see their parents. It is hard to imagine this degree of cruelty. Yet the administration decrees it, the courts confirm it, and public opinion—which, years ago, stopped having the least human empathy for Palestinians, even children—accepts it.

Systematic dehumanization of a colonized people inevitably leads to dehumanization of the colonizers and their society. The Israeli soldiers and settlers, who enjoy complete impunity, as well as the brutality of the prevailing political discourse, have already contaminated Israeli society. Like pollution, violence does not stop at the Green Line. Israeli crime statistics, particularly the figures on domestic violence, prove it. In two years' time the number of assaults and murders increased by over 20 percent. Not a day goes by without the papers reporting serious incidents, especially among young people. Young Israelis today have two role models: the soldiers, whose brutality is presented in the media as heroism, and the settlers, whom Barak calls Israel's new pioneers.

During the past decade settlers have acquired the status of superhuman beings, who are no longer subject to any law or institution. They steal their Arab neighbors' land, harvest their olives, push through roads here and close off roads there, block Arab peasants' access to their fields, and organize punitive raids when they are angry. They have the power of life and death over the natives, and even impose their will on the troops who protect them—without whom they would be nothing more than common thieves.

As for the soldiers, whose average age is twenty-one, they are, collectively and individually, in power. They have absolute power over almost four million human beings. For almost three years now, new orders have given the soldiers the powers of police officers, judges, jailers, executioners, and, should the fancy take them, teachers. You can see barely post-pubescent soldiers playing these roles at the dozens of checkpoints that rule the lives of West Bank and

Gaza Strip residents. You have the soldier who, for fear of making a mistake, lets no one pass, not even a mother with a newborn whose papers show that she's just left the hospital and only wants to go home with her baby. You have the soldier who decides to punish an old man for daring to look him in the eyes, and therefore denies him permission to enter Jerusalem to pray during Ramadan. You also have the inevitable "educator," who makes European Commission diplomats spend a half hour under the hot sun because they crossed an imaginary line that a nineteen-year-old corporal had told them not to cross.[8] At the checkpoints the soldiers do not speak Arabic or English or even Hebrew; they howl their onomatopoeian howls while gesticulating with their M-16s.

In December 2001 a group of international observers and I accompanied Mustafa Barghouti, national coordinator of the Palestinian NGOs, to the checkpoint between Jerusalem and Ramallah after the police had freed him after several hours' detention (for having the nerve to organize a press conference in Jerusalem). About 20 yards from the checkpoint a border guard patrol headed toward us threateningly, and the chief shouted something at us.

"What do they want?" Barghouti asked.

"I don't know," I said, 'they're not speaking Hebrew. I think it's Russian."

"Definitely not," he said, "I studied in the Soviet Union, and I know Russian."

We were now face to face with the guards. They were howling at us, but I still didn't understand anything. I demanded that they stop yelling, that they speak to us, and in Hebrew. Suddenly I realized that they *were* shouting in Hebrew—or rather in a sort of Hebrew-military howl, something in between an articulate sentence and a cowboy's shouts at a herd of cattle.

Israeli soldiers spend so much time yelling at natives that they are gradually losing the power of speech. When they go back to civilian life in Israel they have a harder and harder time readjusting.

On can easily imagine the kind of dialogues they have with their parents and partners and, later on, their children.

To understand the degeneration of Israeli soldiers, you have to read and reread Moshe Nissim's monologue published in the weekend supplement of the daily *Yediot Aharonot.* Nissim, whom his buddies in the battalion call "Kurdish Teddy Bear," drove the huge D-9 bulldozer that destroyed the whole center of the Jenin refugee camp for 72 hours without a break.[9] He says:

> Difficult? You must be joking. I wanted to wipe out everything. When the officers gave me an order to destroy a house, I took the chance to destroy lots of other houses. Take my word for it; we didn't destroy enough of them. Three days long I bulldozed, bulldozed. The whole square. I tore apart every house they were shooting from. And to tear them apart I had to destroy lots of others each time. The soldiers warned the people in there each time so they could get out before I got started. But I didn't wait. I'd give the house a really hard blow so it'd collapse as fast as possible. Maybe others weren't as drastic as I was—or at least that's what they say. Don't believe everything they tell you.

> There were a lot of people in the houses when we started knocking them down. I didn't see any houses falling on living people, but if they did, I don't give a shit. I'm sure some people died in those houses, but it was hard to see, 'cause there was tons of dust and we worked a lot at night. I enjoyed seeing the houses collapse, 'cause I know they [the Palestinians] don't care about dying, but destroying a house hurts them more. If anything bothered me personally, it's that we didn't destroy the whole camp.

> I got a lot of satisfaction out of this; I really enjoyed myself. I just couldn't stop. I wanted to keep working all the time, without stopping. After the fighting stopped we were ordered to pull out the D-9; the army didn't want the reporters and photographers to see us working. I fought against them [the officers] so they would let me keep on destroying. I had a great time in Jenin. A wonderful time. It was like I had concentrated the whole

eighteen years when I hadn't done anything [in the army] in three days.
The soldiers came to see me and said, "Thanks Kurd, thanks."

How did Nissim keep going for three days?

You want to know how I kept going for 75 hours without a break? I never
got down off the D-9. I didn't get tired at all, 'cause I kept on drinking
Scotch. I had brought some along in my bag. Everyone else brought
clothes, but I knew what was coming. I brought along Scotch and pista-
chios. Jenin helped me forget my troubles.

Two months before the Jenin massacre, *Independent* war correspondent Robert Fisk wrote that the Israeli Defense Force was no longer a
modern army but rather a collection of armed gangs sacking everything in their path and allowed to pillage Palestinian towns with complete impunity. It even seemed to have lost its operational capacity. It
was getting by by using massive and disproportionate force.

There has always been looting in wars. But in the past in the Israeli
army it was severely punished. In the current campaign of pacification,
vandalism and looting are part of the message that the military and
political leaderships are sending: To crush terrorism, you have the
right to break up everything; in our life-and-death war, all is fair!

In this sense Moshe Nissim is not an extreme case. He is the product of the generalized degeneration of an occupation army, and of a
society that, by totally dehumanizing the adversary, is rapidly losing
everything that made it—despite everything, despite the plundering
and the institutionalized discrimination—a relatively civilized society.
Once Israel's institutions, and specifically the army, had to give an
accounting, had some norms of conduct and a certain conception of
respect for laws and human dignity—all that is disappearing.

These changes would not have been possible without a qualita-
tive shift in the society's dominant discourse, as expressed not only
by political leaders but also by the opinion makers, the media, the
universities, and court rulings and verdicts.

INTERLUDE: THE WALLS' TURN TO SPEAK

Israelis and Palestinians have several things in common. One of them is the way they express their political opinions on the walls, as graffiti or on posters. Israelis also use their cars' rear windows; stickers are fashionable, especially among right-wing currents and the orthodox. Reading what's written on the walls and stuck on cars doesn't give a good picture of public opinion, because moderates tend to be less exhibitionistic. But it does give a good idea of the overall framework within which politics is discussed.

From July to November 2002 I walked around with a notebook and faithfully wrote down in it the slogans I came across. Here I will share the most significant of them, dear reader. Obviously I've had to make a selection, but my selection is entirely typical of what I've seen. I must make one remark, however: I did my little survey mainly in Jerusalem, which is a more right-wing and religious city than the Israeli average.

SOLUTIONS:[1]
Transfer = Peace + Security (a poster pasted up all over in Jerusalem)
Jordan Is the Palestinian State—Transfer Now!
    (hundreds of posters on the freeway from Tel Aviv to Jerusalem)
Deport the Arab enemy (poster)
Deport Arafat! (poster)
Beat the Arabs—Break the Arabs (posters)
No leftists, no bombings (graffiti)
It's them or us—Transfer (posters)
300,000 of them have already left for Jordan—Transfer (posters)
Kahane was right—Kick out the Arabs! (graffiti)
Death to Arabs (graffiti)

ON THE RIGHT:
No to the hostile media! (sticker)
I only buy from Jews (posters)

Put the Oslo criminals on trial (sticker, posters, and graffiti)

Peace is a catastrophe; we want war! (sticker)

No to Perestine! (graffiti)

Hebron Forever (sticker)

ON THE LEFT:[2]

We want peace (sticker)

No Trans-Israel freeway (sticker)

No vivisection (sticker)

Death to the orthodox! (graffiti)

Separation now (sticker)

NATIONAL RECONCILIATION:[3]

Order of Reconciliation (huge billboards and stickers)

Unity—Right Now! (billboards and stickers)

I love Tsahal (sticker)

Congrats, Tsahal! (sticker)

Soldier, you are my brother (sticker)

MORE RIGHT-WING THAN THOU:

Sharon is giving the terrorists a state (posters for the Likud primaries)

Why does the left back Sharon? (posters for the Likud primaries)

JERUSALEM:

Jerusalem, I will be true to you! (sticker)

A Jew does not betray Jerusalem (sticker)

GOD:[4]

We love you, God (sticker)

God is the only one you can count on (sticker)

Our rebbe, our master, may he live forever!

The messiah-king is against a Palestinian state[5] (billboard)

THE HORROR:

Shoah for the Arabs! (graffiti in the Jerusalem bus station)

3. The New Face of Racism

The framework and limits of the prevailing discourse in Israel have changed considerably since the Camp David fiasco, in terms of both content and form. The full seriousness of the degeneration of Israeli society during the past three years appears perhaps even more in open public expressions of racism than in the brutality of the repression in the occupied territories.

By identifying Palestinians in general with terrorism and justifying the policy of pacification in the occupied territories as a life-and-death struggle for Israel's survival, the Israeli political class has opened the floodgates for racism and violence. Every form of restraint and every limit seem to be evaporating. Racism and violence have always been in Israeli culture, admittedly, but generally liberal values and democratic pretensions held them in check.

BRUTALITY WITHOUT BORDERS

As some of the slogans cited on posters and stickers suggest, public expressions of racism are now generalized and legitimized by political parties at the forefront of Israeli political life and represented in the government. The racism revolves around two axes that, taken together, synthesize the new political philosophy in relation to the Palestinian people: repression and deportation.

The brutality of the last few years is rooted in two of human beings' most visceral reflexes: fear and desire for vengeance. Politicians have been fostering and manipulating the fear, in its crudest and most primitive forms, without trying to civilize it at all. The drumbeat is: they want to slaughter you; they are bombing you; we have to strike back without scruples, restraint, or thought for the consequences, even the consequences for Israelis' own safety. As for the desire to revenge the victims, like anywhere else it keeps the whole infernal cycle in motion: you blow yourself up in Tel Aviv, I bomb Gaza; you kill three of my children, I kill five of yours.

But beyond the logic of vengeance, the "preventive" strikes and reprisals have a dual political objective. For the most moderate Israeli politicians—in particular the Labor Party and part of the high command—they are a way to break the back of a resistance that has now lasted more than thirty-five years, and make the Palestinians accept a "solution" that up to the present every current of Palestinian opinion has rejected. For the extremists, the violence in the occupied territories is meant to get the Palestinians to leave—what the Moledet Party calls "voluntary transfer"—or else lead to an escalation culminating in a large-scale ethnic cleansing operation.

The symbol of Israel is no longer the Star of David (called "David's shield" in Hebrew), but rather the bulldozer. Bulldozers are used everywhere, all the time: to push through bypass roads, destroy houses, roads and neighborhoods, uproot trees and orchards; in short, to destroy nature and culture. Once set in motion, the bulldozer does not stop short at the Green Line, either. In Israel itself the bulldozer rules supreme, without any concern for the environment or respect for nature or landscapes. Mountains are disemboweled; the few remaining forests are uprooted. The bulldozer has become the ultimate means of affirming Israeli sovereignty and conquering the land, Cossack-style.

Surrender or get out: this is the choice that the Israeli political-military class, for whom violence has become its only political instrument, offers the Palestinians. It is no accident that the government held no discussion whatsoever on the peace plan adopted

unanimously by the Arab League countries, offering Israel peace
with the Arab world in exchange for withdrawal from the occupied
territories. The Israeli government is not interested in peace any-
more, even with all the Arab countries. Its only interest is in continuing the process of seizing all of historic Palestine.

Ariel Sharon never tires of repeating that his perspective is not
peace but "a 100-year struggle with Arabs."[1] He means to continue
the 1948 war of independence, a war that resulted in Israel's taking
control of almost 80 percent of the territory of Mandate Palestine
and a gigantic campaign of ethnic cleansing. "The war for independence isn't over yet," says Sharon.

> No. 1948 was only a chapter. If you ask me if the State of Israel can defend
> itself today, I say, Yes, absolutely. But do we live in security? No. This is
> why it's impossible to say that we've finished off the job. Evacuating even a
> single settlement is out of the question, because every one of them has a
> strategic value or a Zionist value. It is impossible to end the conflict.[2]

If your perspective is a hundred years' war, then you absolutely
have to glorify the army, which had lost much of its prestige over
the last two decades. In the past three years the army has regained
the place that it occupied until the late 1970s at the heart of the
Israeli nation. Everyone in Israel—or almost everyone—has fallen
lovingly in step behind it. Admittedly, there is a movement of con-
scientious objectors that is far from marginal. But all those who fail
to see the oppressive character of military action in the occupied
territories—meaning the great majority of Israeli society—are now
once more seeing the army as the last bulwark against a new
Auschwitz. What was referred to during the past twenty years as
the "crisis of motivation" seems to have been overcome. The
demand to serve in combat units, among which some of the most
prestigious have turned into real death squads specializing in extrajudicial killings, exceeds the supply of available slots.

Alongside the army, the settlers too have gained a new legitimacy, at the very moment when the violence of their behavior has broken all previous records, thanks to the green light they got from the army high command. Since the beginning of the intifada, the Alternative Information Center has chronicled about twenty murders of Palestinians by settlers, all but one of which have remained unpunished; the investigation always ends in a dead end within the first few days.[3] Settlers build houses and push through roads on Palestinians' land, and shoot at them when they try to work in their fields. The olive harvest, the main activity of a Palestinian peasant family in the fall, has become impossible. Only after several deaths, and only thanks to the solidarity of Israeli and international peace activists, did the Israeli army decide in 2002 to restrain the settlers' murderous zeal.[4] The settlers are fulfilling a biblical curse, by the way: "And thou shalt speak unto him, saying, Thus saith the LORD, Hast thou killed, and also taken possession? And thou shalt speak unto him, saying, Thus saith the LORD, In the place where dogs licked the blood of Naboth shall dogs lick thy blood, even thine."[5] More and more often they are picking the olives themselves, in accordance with a religious verdict handed down by Israel's former chief rabbi Mordechai Eliyahu. Since the land of Israel is the inheritance of the Jewish people, Eliyahu said, the Arabs are thieves; "their olives" are in fact our olives.

Yet without army protection and government support, the settlers are nothing. Their exorbitant power depends on the influence they have managed to gain inside the national institutions, army, and government. They have become one of the country's most powerful lobbies, recalling in many waves the power the kibbutzim had in the 1950s and '60s. As a member of the European parliament on a delegation to the occupied territories said recently, "The settlers are your OAS, but an OAS that has taken power."[6]

DELIRIUM

Nothing is less of a sure thing, however, than the success of the bloody campaign of pacification in the occupied territories. Despite martial law, the bombings, all the dead and wounded, the massive destruction and the blows to the civilian and military institutions of the Palestinian Authority, nothing suggests that the Palestinians are about to give up. The determination of the Palestinians of every political and religious current is expressed in their stubborn persistence in staying put and going on with normal life in the midst of the destruction. We see it in their efforts to keep the educational system functioning, at whatever cost—and sometimes it costs schoolchildren's lives; the miracles worked by municipal employees in restoring what the Israeli troops have vandalized; and the courage required to get through the shutdown in order to get to work, visit a sick grandmother or get a dialysis treatment at the hospital. All these efforts are acts of popular resistance, which Sharon is not managing to break.

But like all the beribboned blockheads in the world, the Israeli generals, including those who have taken off their uniforms to become cabinet ministers, are convinced that what they have so far failed to achieve by use of force can still be achieved by using more force.

If the shutdown does not produce the hoped-for results, then they impose a curfew, for five weeks if necessary, as in Nablus. If rockets launched from Apache helicopters do not seem to "put an end to terrorism," then they send out F-16 fighter jets, armed with one-ton or even heavier bombs. If five militants rise up to take the place of every militant the army murders, then it's time to kill Yassir Arafat. Assassinating the president of the Palestinian Authority— sometimes referred to in code as "expelling" him—has become the obsession of all the politicians who have ended up to Ariel Sharon's right, because this seems to be the only limit that George W. Bush has imposed on the Israeli prime minister.

What will they think of next in their escalating series of measures to put an end to terrorism: eradicating the Palestinian Authority, deporting terrorists' families, razing their villages, selective or wholesale transfer? Most worrying is that the Sharon government is not just engaged in a verbal game of more-violent-than-thou but in a step-by-step application of concrete, real measures. What seemed improbable yesterday is carried out today. This is why, as former Jerusalem deputy mayor Meron Benvenisti has explained, we have to take the "worst-case scenario" very seriously.[7]

A political class that feels no particular qualms about discussing the worst possibility is quite capable of moving from words to deeds, whether this means deporting Palestinians en masse, destroying Jerusalem's mosques, or using nuclear weapons. The fact that these possibilities are even being discussed shows that there is no longer a foot on the brake. Ephraim Halevi, former head of the intelligence agency Mossad and Sharon's security adviser, recently said in front of an audience of specialists:

> A successful mega-attack would immediately lead to a radical change in the rules of Israeli behavior. The essence of the threat hovering over us is genocide, the eradication of the country and the destruction of its foundations. Faced with such threats, Israel has a diverse and varied range of measures at its disposal that it is preferable not to discuss in advance. We can reasonably suppose that international public opinion will understand and accept the shift in the rules of the game and our modalities of action.[8]

As for Sharon, during the summer of 2002 he threatened to drop a nuclear bomb on Iraq if Saddam Hussein dared to attack Israel with nonconventional weapons, adding, "even if there wasn't a single Israeli victim." It goes without saying that using Israel's nuclear potential, whose very existence the country's leaders had denied until then, would sign Israel's death sentence; the whole of the Arab and Islamic world would rise up against it.

One might say that this type of threat is part of a classic strategy of deterrence. But there are people in the Israeli government for whom, in the pre-messianic era we are now in, nuclear war including its countless victims is all part of God's plan, which will lead in time to the establishment of the reign of Israel's God over the earth. So the game is worth the candle.

There is an explosive, suicidal mix of people at the head of the state of Israel today. It includes military brutes like Generals Shaul Mofaz and Moshe Yaalon, extremist nationalists like Avidgor Liberman and Uzi Landau, irresponsible adventurers like Benjamin Netanyahu, and messianists like Rabbi Beni Eilon and General Efi Eitam. The pen of the extreme religious fringe and the sword of atomic weaponry sit side by side in this cabinet. Given this speedy rightward drift of the Israeli political class, one can understand that the Israeli public no longer sees Sharon as the extreme right-wing general and war criminal that he was (and still is), but rather as the moderating element in his governmental coalition, at the center of the Israeli political spectrum.

Messianic nationalism and militaristic messianism require us, as Meron Benvenisti has warned, to consider the worst-case scenario as a real option, and the apocalypse as a concrete political project.

THE PERVERSE RETURN OF THE SHOAH

By presenting the colonial war from August 2000 on as a life-and-death struggle for Israel's survival, Ehud Barak conjured up the demons that haunt the collective memory of the Israeli people. It began with an editorial by journalist Ari Shavit in the daily *Haaretz*, about the first stones that young Palestinians threw in response to Ariel Sharon's provocative visit to the Al-Aqsa mosque. Shavit, one of many intellectuals on the Israeli left who renounced all their beliefs about peace within a few weeks, wrote that the problem is not the Israeli-Palestinian conflict and the occupation after all, as he had wrongly believed for too many years. The problem (Shavit wrote) is rather what he called the "Jewish fate": eternal war for survival in a world that has always rejected the existence of Jews and will continue to do so for all eternity. This line of argument, passed from one media outlet to the next and adopted by the majority of Israeli intellectuals, is rooted in a profound existential angst in post-Auschwitz Jewish consciousness. But the fallacious way that history is taught in Israeli schools lends it credibility. Israeli schools reduce two thousand years of Jewish history to one vast pogrom and a timeless, irrational, and unique anti-Semitism, thus making any attempt at understanding and any effort to fight anti-Semitism futile.

For the grandchildren of the victims of the Nazi genocide, any existential threat, real or imaginary, is associated with Auschwitz and Treblinka. The Palestinians are Nazis; Arafat equals Hitler; an ambush where soldiers are killed is a massacre; and a bomb in Tel Aviv is Kristallnacht. With associations like these, any possibility of negotiation or compromise evaporates. Nazism in its Palestinian form must be eradicated, and any means is legitimate.

Yet Israelis do recognize on some level that the equation between Palestinians and Nazis is fallacious. Israel's military power and crushing advantage over the Palestinians make it a bit difficult for Israelis to identify with the wretched Jews of Warsaw and Vilna, or even with the Warsaw Ghetto fighters or the Jewish partisan units in the Belarussian forests. The result is a horrible, perverse mental gymnastic. The continual references to the genocide of the European Jews and the omnipresence of those terrible images lead to a situation where, since the reality of the relationship of forces prevents Israelis from mimicking the behavior of the Jewish victims, they adopt, in general unconsciously, the behavior of those who slaughtered the Jewish people. They tattoo Palestinians' arms, make them run naked, confine them behind barbed wire and prison camp watchtowers, and even briefly used German shepherds to control them.

The house-to-house sweeps in the Deheisheh camp could not help evoking another historical period, even though of course the Palestinians picked up in the raids were not being sent to their deaths but rather to unlimited detention in horrible conditions. The Offer detention camp is not an extermination camp; but it closely resembles the German concentration camps of the 1930s, with its barbed wire, watchtowers, and masses of frightened prisoners destitute of rights and confined in truly inhuman conditions. How can one help seeing that a row of Palestinian civilians with their hands in the air filing past a guard of armed soldiers is a reproduction of the haunting image of Warsaw's Jews on their way to the Umschlagplatz? How could one not be reminded of that same Umschlagplatz when the television broadcast images of hundreds of men in Jenin, sitting on the ground, their hands tied behind their backs, some of them blindfolded?

The vocabulary is also a Nazi vocabulary. Consider the article that Rabbi Israel Rosen wrote for *Haaretz,* in which he said that the families of suicide bombers must be taken hostage and deported to Gaza, and then their houses must be leveled and their villages razed. The Israeli journalist B. Michael cited statements identical to Rabbi Rosen's by Nazi officers after the Lidice and Oradur massacres, ending his article:

> And if there are people out there who insist on concluding from what they've just read that I'm comparing the Israeli army to the German army— God forbid—then they're making life too easy for themselves. It's the man who proposed [this] to the Israeli army that came up with the equation.[9]

A few days after the media reported that Palestinians were having numbers tattooed on their arms, Michael, himself the child of survivors, published a harsh, painful article with the title, "From Tattooed to Tattooer":

> The historical path that the Jewish people have traveled during the past 60 years that divide 1942 from 2002 could doubtless provide material for fascinating historical and sociological studies. In 60 short years: from tattooed and numbered to tattooer and numberer. In 60 years: from prisoners in ghettos to imprisoning others. In 60 years: from filing by in columns with our hands in the air to making others file by in columns with their hands in the air.... It's been 60 years, and we've learned nothing, internalized nothing. We've forgotten everything...! Finally! We are no longer a different, strange people, with pale faces and looks filled with wisdom; we're brutal soldiers like all the others. Finally we are a nation like unto other nations.[10]

I just wrote "in general unconsciously." But sometimes this perverse mental gymnastic is entirely conscious. Consider the example of the high-ranking Israeli army officer who explained to his troops as they were about to invade the Palestinian refugee camps that they had to learn from others' experiences, including the way the German troops took control of the Warsaw Ghetto.[11] This was a Jewish soldier, perhaps the grandson of a victim of the Nazi genocide, who wanted to learn from the Germans' success in slaughtering more Jews, in order to apply the lessons against the Palestinians! There are leading figures of the French Jewish community who support Jean-Marie Le Pen, and others who welcome the beneficial effects of Le Pen's electoral success![12] One leader of the Representative Council of Jewish Institutions in France suggested using Goebbels's propaganda methods to make pro-Israeli propaganda more effective! Is there a greater perversity imaginable than this?

4. The Wall

If, as Ari Shavit says, the Palestinian struggle is only one link in the desire of all nations, everywhere and forever, to eradicate the Jewish people, then the Jews need to wage their war for survival on a planetary scale. Then the Palestinians will be only the shock troops of a worldwide anti-Semitic offensive, not only Muslim but Christian as well as leftist. Arafat, Bin Laden, Chirac, and Naomi Klein are all on the same side. Anti-Semitism is everywhere, and the foul beast is coming out of the lair where the horrors of Nazism had forced it to hide.

A NEW GHETTO

Israelis' anxiety about a global anti-Semitic offensive, even if to some extent the product of a cynical campaign carried on by the country's rulers and their lavishly paid PR agents, is real. Any anti-Semitic incident, or as is often the case any incident interpreted as anti-Semitic, is immediately perceived as the signal for a pogrom. French philosopher Alain Finkelkraut, champion trivializer of the Holocaust, does not hesitate, for example, to speak of a "Kristallnacht year" in France. The Israeli media of course pick up and amplify this kind of statement, reinforcing still more a psychosis that is spreading like an epidemic. When one of my nephews, an observant Jew, visited France recently, he had his rabbi's permission to go out without his yarmulke; he would risk death if he appeared publicly in France as a Jew, he said.

We will come back to the extremely dangerous effects that this kind of worldview has on Jewish communities in the Diaspora.[1] In Israel, it has tragic implications.

Faced with a world that it sees as (almost) totally anti-Semitic, Israel can no longer engage in a dialogue with international public opinion, whether it is right-wing, left-wing, pro-Palestinian, or even motivated by a sincere concern for Israel's future. Looking through the distorting prism of anti-Semitism, Israelis see any criticism, even the most moderate, as monstrous. When these criticisms come from prominent Jews, Israelis see those who make them as at best irresponsible, criminally blind to the imminent danger, and at worst as traitors motivated by "self-hatred."

With the world a hostile, dangerous jungle, Israel has reacquired ghetto reflexes. These are not the medieval (and later Nazi) ghettoes imposed on Jews, but rather voluntary ghetto reflexes, the kind that rabbis wanted to maintain at all cost in order to neutralize outside influences.

Beginning in the summer of 2001, for instance, the minister of the interior instituted a policy meant to block entry to Israel by anyone suspected of having reasons other than family visits or tourism. In the ensuing year and a half, according to *Haaretz,* almost 10,000 people, members of delegations in solidarity with Palestinian people as well as others, were forbidden to enter Israel. A little more than a thousand others were expelled (not counting the thousands of immigrant workers without valid papers).[2] All foreigners who arrive at Israel's frontiers are ipso facto suspect and subjected to searching interrogation about what brings them to Israel. The Israeli authorities seem aware that Israel is not a place that a normally constituted person would want to visit, the way one visits London or Katmandu.

Haaretz recently devoted the central article in its weekly supplement to this subject, under the title, "Our Fortress Is Closed." Sara Leibovitz-Darr describes in the piece how, over the course of two years, thousands of artists, athletes, journalists, or ordinary tourists were turned back, particularly if they were black or had Arab names. "There used to be holes, but we've closed them," said the minister of the interior. Dani Sieman, director of the government press office, was more straightforward:

> Up until know they [foreign journalists] knew that they could tell us any old story, because we were sensitive about our image. Now we've stopped bothering ourselves about what they might write about us. If they don't write about the fact that we didn't let them into Israel, they'll write about something else. You know what kind of people come here? Pro-PLO types. Who needs people like that?[3]

Interior Minister Eli Yishai added, "If a journalist comes to throw mud at Israel, and we have information on him, then we don't let him in."

On the subject of people suspected of "pro-Palestinian positions," the ministry of the interior makes no bones about the motives behind its policy of closing the borders. On several occasions it has declared in court that it would block entry into Israel by anyone with "pro-Palestinian positions"—and that leaves room for a wide variety of interpretations. "I won't let people like that strengthen terrorism at a time when we're at war," the minister concluded.[4]

Judge Moshe Drori responded, in a verdict concerning a group of young French Communists who had been forbidden to enter the country, "In my opinion, a general policy that considers all people coming from abroad guilty fails to distinguish between good and bad."[5] Earlier during the same trial he spoke of the risk of xenophobia and the danger for the country of turning in on itself.[6] Three days later the High Court overturned Judge Drori's decision.

Yet Drori was right: Israel is prey to a growing xenophobia and caught up in a logic that assumes—as a famous Israeli children's song says—that "the whole world is against us." When Ehud Barak says that "Israel is a villa in the heart of the jungle," he is of course

expressing a racist attitude toward the surrounding Arab environment, defined as a space of barbarism and violence.[7] But one can
also detect in his words a ghettoization of Israel from the whole rest
of the world. This is the ideological and cultural backdrop that
enables us to understand the new Israeli delusion about the "separation fence," better known to the rest of the world as "the wall."

UNILATERAL SEPARATION

One element of the new Israeli consensus is that we have to build a
wall "between them and us." The great majority of Israelis support
this project, as does the whole political class—except for part of the
extreme right.[8] Some politicians, like former Labor minister Haim
Ramon, have made it the entire content of their political program
and electoral campaign.

For Israel in 2004, the wall means safety. People only feel safe
behind walls. The idea of a wall may seem paradoxical for a country that has always refused to define its borders. But it is part and
parcel of the inherent logic of Zionism and the spirit of "we are
here, they are there" that underlies this ideology. For Zionists from
Herzl and Pinsker in the late nineteenth century up to Rehavam
Zeevi and Haim Ramon, the only normal society is an ethnically
homogenous society. Excluding those who are different, racism
(and therefore anti-Semitism) are natural phenomena that express
society's need to expel any alien element. This makes the concept
of separation a central one.

One of the most widespread posters in Israeli cities and on Israeli
roads proclaims: "Us here, them there—Transfer!" Activists of the
Labor left have erased the word *transfer* and replaced it with
"fence."[9] But "us here, them there" is the heart of the Israeli consensus. As the far right repeats all the time, its only difference with the
left is where to locate the border between them and us: at the Jordan
River or in the heart of the Land of Israel.

But the wall is not a border:

> It is necessary to make a conceptual differentiation between a reality
> coded as "unilateral retreat" (which means that Israel is unilaterally giving
> up its *de facto* sovereignty over the OPT), and the concept of "unilateral
> separation" (whereby Israel attempts to maintain sovereignty *de facto* over
> the OPT, but creates political and physical conditions to isolate/separate
> the Palestinian population from Israel). As a matter of fact, a unilateral
> retreat by Israel means defeat for the Israeli colonial project, while unilat-
> eral separation is an attempt to suppress the Palestinian uprising.[10]

As early as October 2000 Ehud Barak threatened to impose unilateral separation. According to Ron Ben Yishai, a journalist close to
military circles, separation would have four objectives: ensuring the
safety of Israeli civilians; preventing the Palestinians from taking
any political initiative outside the negotiated framework; a harsh
shutdown that would exact a high price from the Palestinians for
rejecting Barak's offer; and encouraging the Palestinians to restart
negotiations from a weaker bargaining position.[11] If we are to
believe Ben Yishai, Labor's "unilateral separation" was part of a
policy combining negotiation with *Diktats*; and the line of the separation fence was supposed to more or less follow what the Barak
government considered the borders of the new Palestinian state.

The planned wall—also called "separation space"—that the government of national unity decided on in 2002 is different. It is above
all a security project, and in no way is meant to draw any line of
demarcation between an enlarged Israel and a Palestinian entity.

There are nonetheless people inside the Likud—including
Sharon himself—who advocate creating Bantustans in 40–45 percent
of the West Bank. In their eyes the line of the wall could serve as Ban-
tustan "borders" in certain areas. When the Bantustans have been
created and a vast ethnic cleansing operation has cut the number of
Palestinians living outside their walls to a minimum, then the zone of
separation now under construction would be destined to disappear.

THE WALL AND THE BOMB

Construction of the separation fence began on June 16, 2002, in the extreme northern West Bank, a few hundred yards in from the Green Line. It continues 78 miles to the Trans-Samarian Highway, more or less at the latitude of Tel Aviv's northern suburbs. The width of the security zone on the two sides of the electronic fence is at least a hundred yards and often much more. All Palestinian property in this zone is being expropriated and everything inside it, including houses and crops, destroyed. The fence itself is on average nine feet high, equipped with electronic gadgets, flanked by two roads for military patrols, and paralleled by a twelve-foot ditch.[12]

Farther south, alongside the town of Qalqilya, a wall replaces the fence. It is seventy-five feet high and crowned with watchtowers. Here too there are patrol roads and a twelve-foot ditch following the wall's path. In the Jerusalem area a 14-mile-long separation zone is being built, combining fences with walls.[13]

By now most of the wall planned for the northern West Bank has already been built, together with much of the wall in the Ramallah and Jerusalem areas. The estimated cost is $800,000 a mile, for a total of over $300 million for 403 miles of wall.[14]

Beyond the amount that the Israeli (and U.S.) taxpayer will pay for the wall, the cost to the Palestinian population is enormous. An estimated 17,000 dunams (4,200 acres) of land will be expropriated to build the fence and wall. Fourteen villages will be isolated between Israeli territory and the wall; while residents on the Israeli side of the line of separation will not be authorized to enter Israel, they will at the same time have enormous problems trying to enter the West Bank, on which they will remain wholly dependent for school, work, urban services, etc. Twelve other villages, from Salem in the north to Qalqilya in the middle of the West Bank's western border, are already closed off on the eastern, West Bank side of the separation zone, while most of their fields are closed off on the western side and can therefore no longer be farmed. From an agricultural point of view construction of the wall is a genuine national catastrophe, since this area is the real market garden of the West Bank.[15]

But price, whether Palestinians or even Israelis have to pay it, seems to be no object, for two reasons. First, according to the current Israeli consensus, security is an absolute imperative that justifies every crime as well as every sacrifice. Today nothing makes Israelis feel safe except a dual confinement, of Palestinians and of Israelis themselves.

Second, the wall has become the very essence of Israel's phantasmagoric self-conception: a world where everyone is confined at home, "us where we belong and they where they belong" (or rather, where we say they belong). The higher the walls, the better people feel.

Menachem Klein, a liberal political scientist and adviser to the Israeli delegation at the Camp David summit, has written quite accurately:

> The enthusiasm for unilateral separation is reveals not only a crisis of means, but also a crisis of mentalities. This kind of project depends on a mentality consisting of both Zionist voluntarism and unilateral action, of both confinement behind what Jabotinsky[16] called an "iron wall" and the exercise of force outside it. Arabs' "voluntary agreement [to Jewish settlement] is out of the question," Jabotinsky wrote in 1923. "Zionist colonization ... can, therefore, continue and develop only under the protection of ... an iron wall which the native population cannot break through." What can this kind of consciousness mean for the left—which should have a political logic, not a logic of force—for a left that would view the Palestinians as equals and seek a partnership with them rather than seeking to subjugate them? [17]

The irony of history is that Zionism, which wanted to topple the ghetto walls, has created the biggest ghetto in Jewish history. It is a ghetto armed to the teeth, admittedly; a ghetto capable of constantly extending its territory. But it is a ghetto just the same, turned in on itself and convinced that everything beyond its walls is a jungle: a congenitally, irremediably anti-Semitic world with no other goal than wiping out Jewish existence in the Middle East and throughout the world.

When Ariel Sharon called on French Jews to pack their bags and flee Europe, which he said was still anti-Semitic and potentially genocidal, all he had to offer them was a big bunker armed with vast paranoia and nuclear bombs. The combination of paranoia and nuclear weaponry constitutes a mortal danger, not only for the Arab peoples surrounding Israel but also for the Israeli people themselves, above all at a time when the notion of preventive war is spreading like gangrene through the international political arena. There can be no doubt: an Israeli nuclear first strike—which as we have seen the general/ministers Sharon and Eitam will not rule out—would ultimately be a death sentence for the Jewish presence in the Middle East. And it would most likely lead to an anti-Jewish wave of unprecedented proportions throughout the world.

5. Counter-Reformation

During the 1988 Knesset campaign, the former army chief of staff, General Raphael Eitan of the far-right Tsomet Party, used to say that if he was invited to join the new government he would not ask for either the ministry of defense or the ministry of police but the ministry of education. Journalists rather enjoyed questioning him about this odd ambition, since they knew that this peasant general was more of a kulak ignoramus than an intellectual. Even in the officer caste of the time he was one of the least educated. But Eitan always gave the same answer: peace is an illusion; sooner or later we'll be in a real shooting war again; the young generation is fed up with war and is dreaming of a normal life, but it's mistaken, our priority has to be to reeducate young people in the spirit of 1948 and regenerate their virile, combative spirit.

Ariel Sharon and some of his ministers share the old general's point of view completely. The sacrifices that a return to 1948 requires mean a "reeducation of Israeli society, which has acquired a taste for peace, security, prosperity, and the beginnings of normality during the last two decades."[1] This society therefore had to be prepared for the years of war to come, meaning "a real cultural, ideological, legal, and institutional counterreformation."[2] Inevitably, Israel's Arab citizens have been the first to experience this counter-reformation.

PUTTING ARAB CITIZENS BACK IN THEIR PLACE

The slaughter of dozens of young Palestinians in the West Bank and Gaza in the days following Barak and Sharon's provocation at the Al-Aqsa mosque led to a wave of anger among young Palestinians in Israel.[3] Massive demonstrations were organized in the Arab towns and villages of Galilee and the Triangle.[4] In several places young people built barricades on the roads that passed near their villages. The major Hedera-Afula highway was closed for more than a day. Some Jewish settlements in Galilee were encircled for several days, with their terrorized residents not daring to leave their homes.

The radicalism of Palestinian protests in Israel was not only a result of the images of bloody repression in the occupied territories that the television networks showed every evening. It also reflected the enormous frustrations of young people whom Yitzhak Rabin had promised several years earlier—and actually begun to carry out—concrete measures aimed at reducing the structural inequality they have experienced for fifty years. With first Benjamin Netanyahu's and then Ehud Barak's coming to power, young Palestinians had seen their hopes of change melt like snow in the sun.

This double anger fueled a week of radical demonstrations, where the only weapons were the stones that young people were throwing at the police. The police's reaction was unprecedented. In the course of one week, bullets killed thirteen "Israeli Arab" citizens, several were killed in cold blood, dozens were seriously injured, and there were hundreds of arrests.[5] Along with the police repression the Arab population had to defend itself against veritable pogroms. Groups of young Jews literally went Arab-hunting in Israeli towns. Several mosques were attacked, in particular in Tiberias and the Hassan Beck mosque in Jaffa.

The "October 2000 events," to use the phrase that became standard in the Israeli media, or the "October massacre" as Palestinians refer to those days of bloodshed, were a watershed in the Jewish state's recent history. After more than three decades of limited but real progress toward legitimating its non-Jewish population, the Israeli government reconfirmed in blood that even if Palestinians have Israeli identity cards and passports, they are not citizens, not even second-class citizens, but enemies. If they exercise their rights as citizens to demonstrate and protest, their actions are treated as an enemy uprising. The Green Line does not really divide Israel from the occupied Palestinian territories, but rather divides Jews from Palestinians, whatever the Palestinians' formal legal status.

The hysterical, hate-filled press campaign against the so-called Arab riots announced from early October 2000 on that it was time to put the Arabs back in their place.[6] Once more Israel had been too generous, the press said. The Palestinians were a fifth column inside Israel, a dagger waiting to plunge into its back. The right pulled out all the stops, and left-wing intellectuals too were angry: not at the police agents who had fired live ammunition at protesters, nor at the government that had ordered them to treat its own citizens like enemies, but at the ingratitude (once again) of Israel's Palestinians. They had been on the verge of winning at least some of the rights that they had been denied for fifty years, and they had spoiled everything that the left had won for them.

In this kind of atmosphere, the national commission of inquiry that a large-scale Palestinian mobilization had forced on Barak was, understandably, rapidly transformed into a Star Chamber investigating the victims and their leaders. In fact, no inquiry commission was needed to identify the people responsible for the October massacre; Barak and his minister of internal security, Shlomo Ben-Ami, had given orders to break up the movement by all means necessary. The police commander in the northern region, Alik Ron, was a notorious racist; Arab leaders had been demanding his resignation for years because of his calls for a tough policy against the Arab population and its elected officials. But the Barak government was most responsible of all, because of the devastating rhetoric it unleashed after the Camp David fiasco: the equation Arabs = destruction of Israel = enemies.

From October 2000 on, fear descended on both communities. Jews stopped coming to Arab villages and neighborhoods to eat hummus on Saturdays. When Arabs have to be in Jewish towns, for work or other reasons, they huddle in the shadow of the walls. Chases and attacks on Arab passersby have become routine. "Attacks on Arabs in Jerusalem," *Haaretz* reported on November 25, 2002; "A student has to leave school after being stabbed." The article mentions about ten cases of Arab students whom young Israeli hooligans had attacked in the street during November 2002 alone. A week later the weekly *Kol Hair* featured the headline, "New Attack on Arabs in Kiryat Menachem Area of Jerusalem."[7]

Between October 2000 and October 2002, almost sixty bills were introduced in the Knesset aimed at "putting the Arabs back in their place." Some of them have already been passed. These laws aim at limiting the political rights of Arab citizens (making it possible to eliminate a candidate or electoral list that "supports terrorism,"[8] lifting the parliamentary immunity of MKs Azmi Bishara and Ahmad Tibi, etc.); limiting their civil rights (forbidding sale or lease of "national lands" to Arabs,[9] and cutting family allocations to Arabs on the grounds that they have not done their military service);[10] or taking away the citizenship of people who have supported or taken part in "terrorist operations."[11]

During the same period, the authorities have restored the practice of holding Arab activists in Israel in administrative detention. Trials for "inciting to insurrection" have multiplied, sparing neither Member of Knesset Azmi Bishara nor the fifteen-year-old high school student who wrote a poem in class. In order to put the finishing touch on the new order, the government has closed down many Arab NGOs and threatened to close down others.

Perhaps even more significant than the laws and policies that state institutions have implemented is the tone the media and politicians use to talk about (and to) leaders of Israel's Palestinian population, including elected members of the Knesset. For the last three years Arab leaders have routinely been referred to on television and in parliament as traitors and foreign agents, and been threatened with being excluded from politics in the near future or even put in jail. Most journalists working for Channel 1 of the public television network replaced interviews with Arab MKs long ago with veritable interrogations, mixing accusations with threats, all of it in a brutal tone that they would never take with any Jewish MK.

In a press statement published in August 2002, the National Democratic Assembly, one of the main political groupings among Israel's Palestinian population—whose right to participate in elections has been threatened—summed up the offensive:

> In recent months we have witnessed an aggravation of the authorities' attitude toward Israel's Arab minority. This is expressed in unprecedented legislation, which puts the very citizenship of members of this minority in question, systematically delegitimates them, and encourages racist treatment of them. All this is creating a dangerous dynamic that risks degenerating into an apartheid regime in the full sense of the word. An atmosphere of this kind is making racism increasingly legitimate and normal. This tendency has to be reversed now.[12]

The Israeli leaders' goal is in fact to reaffirm the Jewish character of the state of Israel, and to return the Palestinian minority to the situation of tolerance under intense surveillance that it lived in from 1948 until the early 1980s.

NATIONAL REVOLUTION

The offensive against the hard-won rights of Israel's Palestinian minority is only one aspect of the wave of reaction that is rolling over the country. In order to "return to 1948" an entire people is being reeducated and its ideology and behavior adapted to a situation of permanent warfare.

This is primarily the task of the ministry of education. When he formed his new government Ariel Sharon was prepared to let the Labor Party have foreign affairs and defense, but not education. He gave this ministry to Limor Livnat, one of the leaders of Likud's ideological right wing.

In the space of a few months Livnat carried out a thorough housecleaning in the school system. Under the motto, "More Zionism, more Bible," she reorganized the curriculum and scrubbed all "defeatist" odors out of the manuals for history and civics instruction. In particular she banned the history textbooks that the Rabin government had introduced a decade earlier, in which the "new historians'" influence was detectible, and eliminated the courses on peace and democracy.[13]

The new minister also decided to encourage employment of rabbis in the public schools in order to strengthen Jewish consciousness and devotion to tradition. Not content with transforming primary and secondary education, Sharon's "political commissar" also changed the makeup of the National Council of Higher Education, making it into a government transmission belt.

During the last three decades, as in many other authoritarian countries, the universities had been centers for free spirits and critical thinking about official ideologies and policies. From 2001 on, Zionist order was restored in academia. Rectors and deans who have not retooled their thinking rightward are aware that a "leftist" image risks costing them a major part of their budgets and governmental subsidies. They therefore refrain from hiring professors who are too decidedly on the left, and at the same time demand that the leftist professors who are still around keep a low profile. Those who refuse risk losing their jobs, whatever their international reputation, as Haifa University political scientist and (new) historian Ilan Pappe knows from his own experience.

In summer 2002 the Haifa University disciplinary council decided to terminate Pappe's contract, although he has an international reputation for his research on Palestine under the British Mandate. The pretext for termination was the public support Pappe had given to a researcher at the university who had written a thesis on the Tantura massacre of 1948.[14] The international support that Pappe received finally did get him his job back. But the "Pappe affair" brought the reality home to more than one lecturer that the university is no longer a safe place for liberals, and that the authorities have no problem with launching a witch hunt against those who refuse to adapt to the new intellectual and moral order.

Alongside the educational system, the world of culture has also adapted to the Zeitgeist. The non-military censors, who had almost halted their activities over the previous fifteen years, went back to work. The film *Jenin, Jenin,* by the famous (Israeli) Arab actor and director Muhammad Bakri, was banned. The Israeli public will also not have the chance (outside of a few art houses and tryout theaters) that European audiences have had to see the Israeli citizen Elia Suleiman's film *Divine Intervention,* which won the Jury Prize at the Cannes Festival.

As for Yaffa Yarkoni, called "the singer of all the wars," she has simply been banned from the airwaves, for the crime of having—moderately—criticized the Israeli army's plundering in the occupied territories. Sylvain Cypel wrote in *Le Monde*:

> The 76-year-old Yaffa Yarkoni was a national landmark: the local equivalent of Maurice Chevalier or Edith Piaf, plus patriotism. Nicknamed "the singer of all the wars," Yarkoni more than any other person poured her energies into keeping up the troops' morale from 1948 to 1982, particularly in the 1956, 1967 and 1973 wars. Thousands of photos have shown this big, handsome woman alongside Israel's most famous generals, from Moshe Dayan to Ariel Sharon. She has received the Israel Prize, the country's highest distinction. In short, she is a living icon. But since April 14 [2002], Yaffa Yarkoni has become a "traitor," boycotted on the air and denounced in the media.[15]

Along with academia, the media had been the second refuge for openness and critical thinking in the 1980s and '90s. It is no accident that one of the right's most popular stickers for years was "No to the hostile media." The media's turnaround during the fall of 2000 was spectacular. Both public and private radio and television networks became agencies of the ministry of defense, mobilized in the service of the war effort. Their critical spirit (often described as "negative," four years ago) has given way to propaganda on command, self-censored and vicious toward anyone who disagrees with the government or the army "reports."

The talk shows have become competitions to see who can be the most militarist and racist. Journalists and commentators considered to be on the left, like Uri Avnery, for instance, are no longer invited. Debates on themes like "Transfer, yes or no?"; "Should we kill Arafat?"; or "Should Arabs be denied the right to vote?" are everyday occurrences on public television screens. In this military and patriotic concert, "experts on Arab affairs" like the unspeakable Ehud Yaari are the bandleaders.[16] Their "analyses" are presented evening after evening in a tone that combines extreme self-satisfaction with ominous theatricality. All they do is repeat the "forecasts" of the various intelligence services, which often contradict themselves from one day to the next according to the fluctuating policies of the government and high command.

The print media, in private hands, is not very different from the broadcast media, although there are still some critical journalists and editorialists who refuse to howl in chorus with the rest of the pack.[17] Many journalists on the left have been fired or seen their scope for publication considerably cut back. The mass-market weekly *Kol Hair* went through an unprecedented upheaval in the fall of 2002; most of the editors in charge of particular departments and almost half of its writers were either dismissed or pushed out. Yet *Kol Hair* was the most popular and profitable publication in the Shoken chain (which publishes the daily *Haaretz*), despite its supposed "leftism."

Since 2001 the media has been stroking public opinion with the grain. It has stopped playing the crucial role it had played during the Lebanon war and the first intifada, when it helped raise the consciousness of the majority of public opinion and helped change government policy.

DEGENERATION

In the space of three years, the norms of collective and individual behavior in Israeli society have changed profoundly. The changes have left no area of public or daily life unaffected. A new normality has taken hold, sweeping aside what was considered normal for the previous twenty years. The "return to 1948" that Ariel Sharon is so dedicated to is not just a choice about policy and military tactics but also a choice for a particular kind of society, which is being implemented here and now.

The attacks in Israeli cities have necessitated security measures that are a constant feature of daily life. Police checks and checkpoints have become a permanent reality in Israel. The police presence in towns and on the highways is massive. Armed guards watch over movie theaters and department stores, schools and restaurants, bars and buses. No one can enter a public place without submitting to a more or less thorough frisking. Suspicion is everywhere. This means that anyone with even a slightly dark skin (that is, close to half of the Jewish population) is subjected to special, often aggressive scrutiny.

The most surprising thing is that people adapt to these omnipresent security measures as if it were a natural phenomenon, and to a large extent as if it were expected. Not only do people not protest; they accept this abnormal normality with apparent feelings of approval. It is as if they are returning to a well-known role that they had been deprived of for too long.

Yet inevitably all these security precautions have serious repercussions for the whole of society, and not only in financial terms. The atmosphere fosters not only paranoia but also violence. First the police and then private guards have begun to abuse their power more and more, reproducing in Israel the behavior characteristic of the checkpoints and controls in the occupied territories. Their language has become more and more aggressive and rude; fiat has been replacing law. This is to be expected; in a state of war, those who are in charge of security have more and more power. They are above ordinary citizens and, increasingly, above the laws. Citizens find this natural, and thus give up their rights as citizens.

This degeneration of norms of conduct and decline in respect for the law has been spreading at every level. Any police officer can now short-circuit the right to demonstrate or leaflet. If you say that these are rights that have been recognized for years, guaranteed by High Court decisions, he will respond simply and in general quite crudely that High Court decisions mean nothing to him.

This steadily greater contempt for the law is not only characteristic of the military administration in the occupied territories, but increasingly of the Israeli civil service. For years now police and prosecutors have been "forgetting" to contact lawyers. When it suits them the officers in charge (usually twenty-year-old lieutenants) just hang up on lawyers who persist in wanting to see their clients. Appeal procedures are ignored, including in the case of civilians expelled by the ministry of the interior. While in the past officials respected individual rights—or at least paid some attention when rights were mentioned—their tendency today is to ignore them.[18] One lawyer told me recently that when he was trying in vain to have a measure revoked that was obviously illegal and asked the police officer to identify himself for an appeal to his superior officer, he was told, "Go fuck yourself." This kind of behavior was rare five years ago. Today it is becoming the norm.

High Court decisions are increasingly turning the norm into the law, moreover. The High Court too used to be known for its (relative) openness and liberalism. Readers may remember its 1999 decision to forbid every form of torture, for instance, or its decisions authorizing appeals of all administrative measures such as house destructions and expulsions. In the last two years the court has once again ruled that torture is permissible; appeals have been drastically restricted; and the rights of people under arrest have been cut back to what they were in 1967–69. The High Court as well has put its uniform back on and gotten in step with the state of war.

This militarization of state and society has serious consequences for social norms: a new increase in daily domestic and public violence; disappearance of the last signs of civility in human interactions; and more and more open corruption among the political class. To give one last example: the primary elections for the Likud candidates for the Knesset took place in such glaring conditions of corruption, extortion, and vote-buying that the police felt obliged to open an investigation. A particular concern is the open role of the mafia in Likud primary elections. (The same is doubtless true in other parties.)[19] It cannot be ruled out that notorious organized crime figures will soon be sitting in the parliament of the State of Israel.

Without critical media, without a High Court ensuring respect for basic individual rights and democratic norms, with an educational system whose mission has become militarizing society and with omnipresent police surveillance, Israeli society no longer has the brakes to stop it from sliding down the slippery slope from the rule of law to a gang culture ruled arbitrarily by violence. The arbitrary rule of violence in the occupied territories is already spreading like gangrene through Israeli society. There is a grave danger that the process of degeneration will speed up in the next few years to the point of changing the state's structures to those of a fascist-type regime that will no longer need to bother about democratic pretensions or the principles of the rule of law.

INTERLUDE: CHRISTMAS IN BETHLEHEM

The Christmas holidays will be observed in the shadow of armored cars "placed at strategic spots in the city in order to prevent terrorist activities," and Bethlehem will be subjected to a tight shutdown.... The fact that our political leaders are incapable, even for a single night, of separating the message of "peace on earth" associated with Bethlehem's Christmas from the brute force that a Merkava tank evokes should be a matter of serious concern to us. This incapacity shows that Israelis are losing little by little what remains of the values that anchor them to the Western, European culture that they claim to belong to.[1] Add to this the worrying developments in the fields of education, immigration, politics and public discourse in Israel, and a feeling of desperation looms. The tank deployed on the Square of the Nativity symbolizes a society that the state of siege and the violent situation in which it finds itself have emptied of all moral sensibility and cultural intelligence, and transformed it into an island cut off from both its geographical and spiritual environments.

—MERON BENVENISTI, former deputy mayor of Jerusalem, *Haaretz*, December 19, 2002

6. A Burdensome Legacy

I have tried in this book's earlier chapters to paint a portrait of a seriously sick society. Israel has to a great extent become a society out of control on a lunatic course. It has lost "all moral sensibility and cultural intelligence," as Benvenisti said. It is destroying everything in its path, including the very possibility of coexisting peacefully one day with the Arab world around it.

We have to ask: How did the state of Israel come to this pass? More specifically, how could this happen after seven years of a peace process that seemed not only to open a new era in Israeli-Arab relations, but also to make possible a normalization of Israeli Jewish society? How could the country slide so quickly into total war and an extreme militarization of people's mentalities and behavior?

Evidently we need to look for the answer to this painful question in the failure of the July 2000 Camp David summit, and the way in which the Israeli public experienced this failure.

THE BIG LIE

After Camp David, Ehud Barak repeated day in and day out, actively backed up by Israel's best-known journalists and most respected intellectuals, that Yassir Arafat's rejection of Israel's "extremely generous offers" proved that the Palestinians had never intended to negotiate a compromise with the State of Israel. Rather, Barak said, the Palestinians had used the negotiations to weaken the Jewish state, and in the long term to destroy it. By saying this Barak not only turned Israeli political life upside down but also transformed Israeli society's perception of its place in the world.

From one week to the next, the country's outlook changed from peace to a life-and-death struggle. Worse, everyone concluded that a plan to eradicate the state of Israel had been concealed for ten years behind a smoke screen of peace. The smoke screen had taken in not only much of Israeli public opinion but also the whole international community—unless, that is, all or part of the international community had been complicit in the Machiavellian stratagem. The new Hitler had been given the Nobel Peace Prize! To cover up his failure at Camp David, as pitiful as it had been predictable, Barak chose to don both Cato's toga and Churchill's top hat: *Palestina Arafatae delenda est,* whatever the cost in blood, toil, tears, and sweat.[1]

"The Left Is Disoriented," headlined the daily newspapers all through the months of August, September and October 2000. Left-wing intellectuals and critical journalists recited their mea culpas one after the other, made their sincere apologies, and swore never to be fooled again by Arabs' talk of peace.[2] This was the time when the greatest Israeli writers, Amos Oz, Abraham B. Yehoshua, and even David Grossman—who would pull himself together a few months later—carried on a campaign in the European media with the theme, "The Palestinian right of return means the destruction of Israel." I will return to this issue, but in this context the message was clear and definitive: the Palestinians want to destroy Israel. The corollary was: We need to defend ourselves, at whatever cost; and faced with the threat of annihilation, preventive war is the best defense. It was Munich 1938 all over again; but we, having learned from the tragic experience of the Nazi genocide, would not let ourselves be caught by surprise a second time. We would destroy the enemy while there was still time.[3]

Two things proved in the eyes of the Zionist left the destructive intent behind the Palestinian strategy. One was the demand for the refugees' right to return; the other was the Palestinian uprising inside Israel in October 2000. With the deafness characteristic of all colonial societies, most Israeli peace advocates had persuaded themselves through a process of self-hypnosis that the Palestinian refugees had already given up the idea of ever returning to their country. Although Palestinian leaders had never stopped talking about the refugee issue for a single day, the Israeli left had stopped listening. It had gradually forgotten that the refugee issue had been explicitly included in the Oslo Declaration of Principles' list of matters to be dealt with in the final phase of negotiations. It saw the Palestinians' request to put the refugee issue on the agenda of the negotiations whose goal was to "definitively and totally put an end to the conflict"—to use Barak's words—as a declaration of war. It proved that "the Arabs hadn't changed at all."

The manifestations of the Palestinians' anger in Galilee in October 2000 was a second sledgehammer blow to all those in Israel who had believed in a process of pacification, in which the Palestinians' main concern should have been to save the Israeli left from falling out with the Israeli right. Even when Israel generously gave them a state, they kept on demanding rights, even inside Israel's own borders! Enough was enough; if they wanted a war, they'd get one.

Once the dynamic of war, and furthermore of life-and-death war, had been set in motion, all the aspects of the current degeneration would follow: consensus, moral collapse, a blackout of dissident opinions, repression first of the residents of the occupied territories, then of Israel's Arab citizens, and finally of the minority of Israelis who denounced Barak's mystifications.

THE WORM IN THE OSLO APPLE

Clearly Barak's big lie played a decisive role in the turnaround in Israeli society. Yet it cannot explain everything. Admittedly, the set of journalists in uniform who dominate the whole Israeli media kept reiterating the same assertions twenty times a day. But the rapidity with which they managed to change Israeli society—its ideology, its behavior, its hopes, and its ethical boundary posts— requires us to look further and deeper to see what made the turn- around possible. No society goes from a massive desire for peace to a resolve for war, from perceiving a neighboring people as a partner to perceiving it as an existential threat, without a major crisis— unless, that is, the turnaround is not as radical as it seems to be, and it had actually begun much earlier.

It was, paradoxically, the Oslo process that brought about a neg- ative change in moderate Israelis' attitudes toward Palestinians. Both Israelis and Palestinians enthusiastically welcomed the announcement of the signature of the Declaration of Principles (DOP) in Oslo in August 1993. Enthusiasm was so great in Israel that several Likud MKs threatened to break party discipline if their party told them to oppose the peace accords. "We'll lose our base if we vote against," they told Likud chairperson Yitzhak Shamir, an indefatigable opponent of any form of compromise.

For several weeks spontaneous fraternization between Israelis and Palestinians spread from one place to the next. There were high hopes that the century-old conflict would end in the relatively near future. Despite the obvious limits and numerous traps contained in the short document signed in Oslo, the DOP seemed to be a point of departure for a process, however long and difficult, of reconciliation between the two peoples. Most of them seemed ready for it.

Nothing was less true. Those among the Palestinians (and the very few Israelis) who persisted through the celebrations with a pessimistic reading of the agreement turned out to be more realistic than the euphoric majority, which talked about irreversibility and about international guarantees to keep both sides to the DOP time line and goals.

The "Peres boys" had had to force Yitzhak Rabin's hand to make him ratify the Declaration of Principles and shake PLO chairman Arafat's hand. Rabin did not believe in peace, at least

not during the first twenty months after the White House ceremo-
ny. The prospect in his eyes was at the very most a new form of
administration for the occupied territories, which would allow
Israel to get rid of Gaza, free up the Israeli army from police work
in the West Bank towns, and above all achieve the long-awaited
separation between Israelis and Palestinians.

After a few weeks of wavering, the occupation army would go
back to its old ways, its repressive methods and its masterful arrogance. The shutdown imposed first on Gaza and then around
Jerusalem would even initiate a new form of repression by seriously
restricting Palestinians' freedom of movement in their own territory. Instead of the economic prosperity that Shimon Peres associated with the Oslo process unemployment went up, due both to the
shutdown and to the obstacles that Israel has put in the way of any
form of investment in the occupied territories ever since 1967.[4]

As for Israel's commitments to "redeploy" its army gradually outside the occupied territories and allow "those displaced in 1967" to
return, they were soon forgotten or revised downward.[5] In short,
Israel dictated its conception of peace to the Palestinians, taking less
and less account of their rights, aspirations, or even existence. Paradoxically, during the first two years of the Oslo process, the Palestinians once again became invisible, in two ways: through the shutdown
and the process of Israeli-dictated peace.

Each time the Palestinians reappeared, either demanding at the
negotiating table that Israel respect the accords it had signed or
carrying out attacks—which increased in proportion to the disap-
pointments and humiliations accompanying the "peace process"—
Israeli public opinion saw them as virtual invaders. What do they
want from us now? was the feeling. After all, we've finally separated
from them, and we've (generously) given them self-rule, guns, and
even the promise of a future state.

While Israelis demanded reconciliation or even love from the
Palestinians as a precondition to any concessions, the Palestinians

apparently had no right to sympathy or even to the respect they had gained earlier by resisting the occupation. For the Israelis, the mutual recognition at the heart of the Oslo accords meant in practice: We recognize your existence, you accept our hegemony, and as for the other open issues, you'll put your trust in our generosity. As proof of this generosity, the Palestinians witnessed during the seven years of the "peace process" a more than 40 percent increase in Jewish settlement on lands that Israel had promised to withdraw from in five years.

But for the Israeli public the essence of the peace process was in place. We were on our land (including the 40 percent of the occupied territories, classified as "C areas," that were gradually becoming "ours") and they were on theirs—shut up in a Gaza Strip increasingly plunged into poverty and in West Bank autonomous areas surrounded by accelerating Jewish settlement.

THE TREASON OF THE INTELLECTUALS

For the intellectuals of the Israeli left, "mutual recognition" played a central role in shaping an ideology that would make it possible seven years later to justify all the crimes against the Palestinians. As soon as the Oslo accords were announced, Israeli intellectuals welcomed the prospect that the Palestinians would stop demanding that Israelis accept responsibility for the 1948 conflict, and more specifically for the *Nakba* (catastrophe) that had created the "refugee issue." For them the PLO's recognition of Israel was not a promise to forgive Israel later for crimes committed in the past, but rather a retroactive certificate of good conduct. It was certainly no accident that the left was the most stubborn in demanding a "letter denouncing terrorism" from Arafat, and that Rabin made it an explicit precondition for ratifying the Oslo accords.

This document, extorted from Arafat 48 hours before the handshake in Washington, was not demanded as a guarantee that the Palestinians would not resort to force; both parties had made a commitment in the DOP itself that they would resolve their differences solely by means of negotiations. The "letter denouncing terrorism" meant for the Israeli left that Arafat was implicitly acknowledging Palestinian responsibility for the conflict. We promise not to be terrorists any more, he was essentially understood as saying, letting it be known that the "hundred-year" conflict had only been a Jewish war of self-defense against Palestinian terrorism.

The peace process was not accompanied by any Israeli self-examination; self-examination was demanded only of the Palestinians. The peace process, far from affecting Israeli society's perception of the conflict, reinforced it. The bad conscience that part of Israeli society had been wrestling with more or less painfully was now stifled, because the Palestinians had supposedly accepted responsibility for the conflict and the crimes that had accompanied it. Israeli peace advocates no longer had to define themselves in relation to the rights the Palestinians had been denied—as they had done during the 1980s. Now it was up to the Palestinians to prove that they were no longer terrorists and were no longer threatening the existence of the Jewish state.

This explains how easily Israelis interpreted peace not as the establishment of justice but rather as a set of new Israeli security arrangements; not as the establishment of peaceful coexistence but as separation. During the years from 1993 to 2000 not one article came from the pen of a major Israeli intellectual that expressed a dream or promised a world of new possibilities. On the contrary, there was an abundance of articles by politician-intellectuals explaining that Israel would now be more secure than before, particularly behind its walls, and anyway Rabin would make sure of the necessary precautions—since you could never be too careful with Arabs. There was no text to serve as the basis for the possibility of a new coexistence among the peoples of the Middle East; no appeal to reexamine our history and change our attitude toward the people who had recently been our enemies—not one.

Equipped with a newly scrubbed good conscience, but also with the same old fear that had afflicted them for the previous fifty years, the Israeli state and society would maintain their own conception of peace, linking separation to reinforcement of hegemony and control.

The Palestinians had seen the Oslo accords as a way of obtaining, if not justice, then at least some of their rights. They knew that those rights would only be granted at the end of five years of negotiations. In the meantime they hoped for an improvement in their living conditions—the economic development that Peres and the IMF bosses had promised—but also the end of the administrative hassles that the military government had imposed. Above all they hoped that Israelis would finally start treating them with dignity and respect.

The shutdown, intensified as soon as the Israeli army carried out its first redeployment, far from improving Palestinians' economic and administration situation, made it worse. They had no more freedom of movement, no more family reunions, no more opportunity to work in Israel, etc.[6] But they could have accepted even this disappointment as an unavoidable detour before obtaining independence and national sovereignty if they had felt at the same time a change in the Israeli civilian and military authorities' attitude: more respect and a less colonial manner. But this was precisely the area in which things went from bad to worse.

FEWER RIGHTS, MORE HUMILIATION

Questioned in 1995 by the BBC's correspondent in Israel about how the Oslo process had changed the military's system of managing the occupied territories, Israeli lawyer Lea Tsemel responded, "It's the same as before, plus some gratuitous nastiness." This kind of gratuitous nastiness is all too familiar to prisoners in the last days of their sentence and soldiers in the last days of their training, when their jailers or sergeants want to show up to the last second that they're still the boss and are not about to tolerate any relationship of equality or any familiarity.

Journalist Uri Avnery, although he had supported the Oslo process with unlimited enthusiasm and optimism, said after the Camp David fiasco:

> It is clear today that the process was bound to fail, because we Israelis were not capable of changing our attitude to the Arabs one bit. It was all still domination, racism, incapacity to treat them as equals—it couldn't work.[7]

Far from giving the Palestinians more rights, including individual rights, the Israeli authorities reduced the Palestinians' rights. They replaced rights with favors, passed out at the negotiating table or granted to those Palestinians with the right friends (or enough money) via notables with whom Israel was in contact. In exchange for the favors, of course, Israelis expected a conciliatory attitude about the still unresolved political problems, and sometimes bribes or fat contracts as well.

Here we see the same paradox again; the Oslo period was the period of the most classically colonial relationship with the natives: favors, a class of go-betweens to manage the occupied population's daily life, and a native police to keep order. The occupation forces divide the class of go-betweens into subgroups with varying levels of privileges depending on the category they belonged to: VIP1, VIP2, VIP3, etc. When one of these privileged people fails to satisfy the superior officer or upper civil servant in charge, he is demoted and thus loses some of his privileges. This or that Palestinian minister loses his permit to travel without being frisked; Arafat loses his helicopter, etc. The Israeli authorities punish Palestinian leaders the way a schoolmaster punishes his pupils, depriving them of free time or a special treat when they don't do what he expects of them.[8]

The colonial relationship also means that the natives are invisible, as became the case after the Oslo process got under way. Apart from the physical disappearance resulting from the expulsion of several tens of thousands of Palestinian workers from Israeli cities and agricultural villages, and their confinement in the hermetically sealed Gaza Strip, the Palestinians disappeared from Israelis' minds. Now they were "on their land," in their state, or what would soon become their state. Even those who continued to work in Israel or live there more or less legally ceased being visible, and therefore ceased being human beings with human rights.

Separation in people's minds occurred before the physical separation and construction of the wall. Between 1994 and 2000 Palestinians stopped being part of Israelis' mental universe. Left-wing intellectuals, who made separation the whole point and primary objective of the peace process, bear an overwhelming responsibility for the Palestinians' disappearance. Imagine their surprise when the Palestinians refused to go away, first by refusing to accept the surrender that Barak—generously—urged on them at Camp David, and then by starting up the resistance again in September 2000.

If even left-wing intellectuals during the auspicious years of the "peace process" perceived peace and the Palestinians in this fashion, we can understand more readily how Barak succeeded so easily in getting Israelis to swallow his lie after the Camp David fiasco, and how the process of dehumanizing the Palestinians went so quickly. They had already disappeared and been wiped out of Israeli reality over the previous seven years. Their return was seen as a veritable foreign invasion and as an aggression against the very existence of Israel. Israelis had seen peace as a commitment by the Palestinian leadership, and as the sole means necessary to stop the violence; so naturally Israelis saw the new wave of acts of resistance as proof of the Palestinian leadership's incapacity or even lack of desire to make peace.

From its own point of view Israel has nothing to reproach itself for and nothing it should change. After all, what greater proof of generosity could there be than what it agreed to give the Palestinians? Therefore Israel had been the sucker in a confidence trick, or rather the victim of a plot. If Barak and Ben-Ami had not uncovered the plot in time, Israel's very existence could have been threatened. From that moment on, anything became permissible.

7. End of an Interval

The speed with which the process of degeneration has been sapping Israel's civic life for the past three years obliges us to look for the roots of the process in an earlier period. Nevertheless, it would be a mistake to deny that a genuine break has occurred in the evolution of Israeli society. We can even date this break: Israel was transformed on the night of November 5, 1995, when religious far-right activist Yigal Amir fired three revolver shots at Prime Minister Yitzhak Rabin. Historians will confirm one day that November 5, 1995, was the moment of the parting of the waters in the history of the Israeli state.

By assassinating Rabin, the far right put an end not only to the possibility of Israeli-Palestinian rapprochement, but also to two decades of normalization and liberalization of Israeli society.[1]

CHOOSING NORMALITY

The Labor Party's 1977 defeat had marked the end of an epoch. During the preceding thirty years, the State of Israel had looked more like an Eastern European "people's democracy" than a Western democracy. There had been a symbiosis between the state and the ruling Labor Party; civil society had been totally subordinated to the state; and the state and quasi-state institutions had controlled all aspects of civic life. There had, however, been one major difference with the Eastern European regimes: the Israeli regime's legitimacy and the country's broad political consensus made democratic

forms possible, at least for those (in the Jewish majority) who iden-
tified with Zionism.

Despite the existence of (relatively) free elections and a certain
margin of political freedom, Israeli society had a totalitarian character in the years 1948–77.[2] The permanent state of war with the surrounding Arab world served as cement for patriotic unity and individuals' voluntary submission to the state. Dissident opinions, sec-
toral struggles, and political criticism were only tolerated within certain clearly defined limits. Anyone going beyond those limits was
slapped down harshly, generally speaking, more by means of social
ostracism than by police methods.

At the end of the 1970s the Jewish state, an uncontested military
power, was experiencing a rate of economic growth that put its living standards around the European average. It had just signed a
peace treaty with Egypt, the most powerful of the Arab countries.
As for the Palestinians in the West Bank and Gaza, they seemed to
have gotten used to the occupation, and to prefer rising incomes to
independence and national sovereignty. The threat that had
loomed over the very existence of the State of Israel since its foundation seemed to be a thing of the past. The future looked glorious.

This new reality put the foundations of the prevailing ideology
and political culture in question, particularly in the world of business and among young people. Israelis wanted to have a normal
society, as in all Western countries. They had had enough of a
mobilized, militarized society.

The individual and individualism became, little by little, legitimate. Doing business and getting rich were no longer shameful
goals that had to be hidden; deciding to leave the country was no
longer seen as betrayal.[3] The word *Zionism* became synonymous
with "retro." Patriotic slogans like "It is good to die for our country"
gave way to "We want to live like everybody else"—"everybody else"
meaning, of course, Westerners. The media and parliament fretted
about the "crisis of motivation" of young people who no longer

fought for spots as volunteers in the elite army units and officer corps. Even those who managed to get themselves classified as unfit for service were no longer stigmatized. The army was no longer the sacred institution it had been during the first three decades of the Hebrew state; reciting the word *security* no longer made people stand to attention the way they had before.

Those were the years in which the "new historians" emerged and began questioning Israel's founding myths. The "new sociologists," who asked questions about the structures of the Jewish state, its particular conception of democracy, and the need to rethink the relationship between a Jewish state and a democratic state, soon followed. More generally, the universities and also the media became hotbeds of critics of Zionism, or at least critics of some of its less democratic aspects. Palestinians, who had previously been absent from the predominant discourse and academic studies, became visible or even central in public debates.

There was no more consensus. Even the most radical critiques of Zionism became legitimate—as did the most openly racist opinions as well, which had previously been inadmissible in public discussion.

Since Israel has no constitution, the High Court assumed responsibility for undertaking a limited but real process of democratizing the state and society. Non-military censorship was abolished in practice; military censorship was put under increased civilian control; freedom of the press was recognized; the right to demonstrate was enlarged; torture was banned; there was even liberal legislation benefiting lesbian/gay couples and decreasing the religious authorities' ability to restrict individual freedom. Even members of the Arab minority won some limited rights; and though structural discrimination against them was not eliminated, a dent was made in it here and there.

The new realities in Israel allowed and demanded that a new balance be found between a "Jewish state" and a "democratic state," as well as between security and individual freedoms: this was in essence the High Court's message.[4] Conservative currents accused the court of carrying out a constitutional revolution that risked de-Zionizing Israel. There was in fact no revolution, but undoubtedly there were reforms.

The decision to elect Yitzhak Rabin in 1992 expressed Israelis' desire to complete the process of domestic normalization by seriously attempting to normalize relations with the Arab world, thereby putting an end to the rejectionist policies of a series of right-wing governments. In the new Middle East that the 1991 Gulf war had ushered in, the prospect of new markets for Israeli capital and technology seemed infinitely more attractive to the new Israeli bourgeoisie than settlements in the West Bank and Gaza. Shimon Peres and his disciples, the "Peres boys," became this bourgeoisie's political spokespeople. They expressed the desire for normalization that animated the secular, liberal middle classes as a whole.

In the eyes of public opinion the Rabin-Peres government symbolized both liberalization of Israeli society and normal relations with the Arab world—implying compromises with the Palestinians to make peace possible. This dual prospect would align against the government all the political and social forces that felt threatened by domestic normalization, Israeli-Palestinian negotiations, or both.

THE FORCES OF RESISTANCE

The right's opposition to the Oslo accords, and its sometimes violent demonstrations against what it called "the Oslo betrayal," are well-known. This opposition was the traditional right-wing parties' doing, but in fact the largely religious settlers' movement led it. They were the ones who demonstrated with signboards showing Rabin in an SS uniform and published a rabbinical "fatwa" condemning the prime minister, declaring that turning part of Land of Israel over to non-Jews was punishable by death.

But this ideological right, which defended Greater Israel and the settlements, was clearly in the minority in Israeli public opinion. In

order to win, it had to ally with all those who were frightened of the
"new Israel"—which some were already calling "post-Zionist,"
extremely prematurely—for whatever reason: religious, identity-
related, socioeconomic, or cultural. Jews of Arab origin felt excluded and marginalized by an increasingly globalized,—i.e., Western-
ized—elite.[5] Orthodox believers saw behind the High Court decisions a desire to "de-Judaize" Israel and challenge the old modus
vivendi between the state and religion. As for the poorest Israelis,
they were seeing the welfare state being dismantled and services pri-
vatized. All these groups felt threatened by the modernization and
liberalization (both cultural and economic) of the state and society.
They made common cause with the right, which was afraid of seeing Israel's patrimony sold off to the highest bidder.

The right's spokesperson Benjamin Netanyahu had a slogan that
expressed perfectly the two dimensions of the coalition that would
defeat Labor's modernizers: "Netanyahu is good for the Jews." The
slogan implied both that the left was siding with the Arabs and that it
was putting the Jewish character of Israeli society in question. The
anti-Labor bloc had a dual objective: on the one hand, to prevent
Israeli withdrawal from the West Bank and Gaza; on the other hand,
to stop the process of opening up that Israeli society was undergoing
and reinforce its specifically Jewish character.

This coalition has gotten more homogeneous over the years. The
secular right has taken on a strong religious tinge, while the fringe
communities (the orthodox and Arab Jews) have gradually adopted
the right's racist, anti-Arab ideology. Rabin's assassin Yigal Amir
represented this synthesis between intensified nationalism and religious fundamentalism. Those who incited him to commit his crime
included both fundamentalist rabbis and far-right politicians.

Assassinating the prime minister was meant to draw a line in the
sand that the right believed should never be crossed. Anyone cross-
ing it was henceforth risking setting off a civil war. At first this
seemed to be a dangerous gamble. Some right-wing leaders clearly

opposed such an extreme step. They feared that the left—that is, the forces who had been working to normalize Israeli society and push onward with a peace process based on compromise with the Palestinians—would take up the challenge and, made confident by its majority support, decide to speed up the dual process of peacemaking and democratization/modernization.

Their fears turned out to be completely groundless. Amir's act turned out to be the most successful bluff in Israel's history since David Ben Gurion's decision to declare the creation of the Jewish state the day the British Mandate forces left. Rarely in the history of political assassinations has a killing so thoroughly attained its goals. Is it an accident that over 30 percent of young Israelis consider killer Yigal Amir a hero?[6]

NATIONAL RECONCILIATION

Shimon Peres, the new prime minister, did not launch a counteroffensive against the right for breaking the rules of the game. Nor did he continue with what people called "Rabin's legacy" after November 5, 1995. Instead Peres undertook a campaign of "national reconciliation." While the right was nervous about the possible consequences of a crime for which it bore much of the responsibility, Peres did not even demand that it apologize, or that it distance itself from its extreme elements. On the contrary, he half accused his murdered predecessor of not having taken enough account of minority opinions and of having pushed the right into a corner. In short, he turned the rape victim into a defendant because she had been shameless enough to go for a walk alone at night.

At the government's initiative, the country was covered with huge posters showing an orthodox and secular Jew together or a "leftist" and a settler together under the slogans, "Time for Reconciliation" or "National Reconciliation." Also at the government's initiative, together with various institutes promoting democracy or dialogue among different (Jewish) communities, more and more gatherings brought together the different components of Israeli Jewish society.

Faced with the arrogance of the right and orthodox believers, the pro-peace, secular majority strained to put forward a coherent politics and ideology. But it was trapped in its contradictions between a Jewish and democratic state and by its desire to pay any price to reconstruct a national consensus. The right sensed that while it was probably facing a majority, it was a majority on the defensive and ready to do anything to make peace with the right. This was the moment to attack; if the "left" wanted reconciliation and consensus, the right could name its conditions.

As for Peres, he chose national reconciliation over reconciliation with the enemy. In order to contribute to this national reconciliation, he slowed down negotiations with the Palestinians. Reversing Rabin's decision, he authorized the assassination of Islamic fundamentalist leader Yihya Ayash, provoking a particularly bloody series of attacks.[7] Then he intensified the Israeli military intervention in southern Lebanon, culminating in the Kana massacre.[8] Peres's approach can be summed up in a manifestly absurd formula: make major concessions to the religious parties in order to win them over to the peace process, and simultaneously slow down negotiations while intensifying repression in the occupied territories and Lebanon in order to reach a political consensus with the right. That was enough to bring the right to power in less than six months: by losing the support of the Arabs and part of the secular left on one side, without gaining anything in the center or in religious milieus on the other, and by creating an atmosphere of insecurity thanks to the fresh wave of attacks.

Rabin's assassin achieved his objective because of Peres's cowardice, his refusal to confront the right, and his deliberate choice to offer up Israeli-Palestinian reconciliation on the altar of Israeli-Israeli reconciliation. By giving in to right-wing blackmail, the Labor Party and its electorate showed that their tribal loyalty was much stronger than their aspiration to peace. They were ready to capitulate unconditionally to the right's values in order to avoid the (in reality very unlikely) chance of a fratricidal war. Decidedly, neither Peres nor Yossi Beilin nor any other Israeli leader, right or left, was going to be the Israeli De Gaulle.[9]

There is an extenuating circumstance in Peres's case: his aspirations for Israeli national unity and his fear of political and ideological confrontation with the right are not unique to Labor Party politicians. They are part of Israeli culture and its prevailing ideology. The peculiar fact remains, though, that the left has lost its capacity since the 1980s to define what the essence of a "Jewish and democratic" consensus should be, while the right is inspired by self-confidence and a nationalist, religious faith that give it certainty that it can set the limits of Israeli identity. The left's reaction to Rabin's assassination only confirmed the right's certainty and strengthened its ideological and political offensive.

From 1996 on, the right's posters and electoral slogans stopped carrying on an ideological battle with the left. Instead they focused on blackmail, threatening a break in national unity with phrases like "A brother doesn't let his brother down" and "Dismantling the settlements would divide Israel down the middle."[10]

By giving up the fight, the liberal, secular left allowed the right to walk away with the 1996 elections. Only a few months before, polls had predicted that the right would be beaten in a landslide. It had been paralyzed by the effects of the prime minister's assassination and what seemed to be a massive mobilization by young people—the ones the media called "the kids with candles," who had mourned for Rabin and democracy on every town square in Israel. In hindsight, this was only the swan song of an Israel that had ceased to exist.

Benjamin Netanyahu had faithfully followed the advice of Arthur Finkelstein, a vulgar, unscrupulous U.S. publicist, and launched a hate campaign against Rabin and the values he had stood for. Following Netanyahu's election victory, the right, in a

period of less than six years, managed to transform the whole ideological and political climate of the state of Israel. The twenty-year
interval of openness, liberalization, and attempts at peace and normal relations with the Arab world came to an end. By assassinating
Rabin the right not only seized political power—including inside
the Labor Party—but also drove the last nail into the coffin of a certain kind of Israel. That Israel gave way to a new kind of country,
with its own particular values and, in the end, a new constitutional
framework and new set of institutions.

INTERLUDE: END OF AN ERA

After having followed the deliberations of the Central
Electoral Commission for several hard, long, bitter days,
I have come to the conclusion that an era has come to an
end in the State of Israel, the era of the rule of law. In
fact, there is no longer a state here at all. A chauvinistic
religious community has launched a life-and-death war,
a tribal war, with neither compass nor conscience, without legal rules, ethical criteria or an ounce of rationality.
I don't believe that Kahane was right, as his disciples'
slogan says; but I'm convinced that Kahane has won.[1]
Not only are his racist theories dominant today in Israeli
society, but his method has triumphed as well: a blend
of chauvinism and religious fundamentalism. If the High
Court upholds the Electoral Commission's decision,
this will be the final liquidation of the concept of Israeli
citizenship, in every sense of the word.[2] We will then
become an apartheid state, a country of lepers in the
eyes of the civilized world. The way is now open to total
war between Jews and Arabs. The majority of the Commission would like to take us back to the era of martial
law[3] and bring Arab collaborators back into the Knesset. If they succeed, their next target will be the activists
of the Israeli left. After ethnic cleansing of Arabs [from
parliament], the next step will be the ideological cleansing of nonconformist Jews.

—HAIM BARAM[4] in *Kol Hair*, January 3, 2003

8. The New Israel

The Central Electoral Commission had to disqualify a party list and two Arab MKs before certain Israeli intellectuals, journalists, and legal experts began asking themselves whether Israel is still even the limited democracy it had been since its founding. The fact that Haim Baram or Uri Avnery ask the question and answer no is particularly significant.[1] Both of them have seen themselves for years as Zionists and Israeli patriots. Baran is what Israelis call a "prince": a son of the country's first pioneers and leaders; Avnery is a hero of the 1948 war, a former MK and celebrated journalist. We are therefore hearing the feeling expressed at the heart of the old Israeli elite that what they thought they had created during Israel's first decades is disappearing, perhaps for good. As Avnery writes:

> Liberman, Orthodox leader Effi Eitam and other Likud leaders are in the vanguard of a fifth column that is laying siege to Israeli democracy. They have begun by inciting their followers to violence against Arab citizens and excluding Arabs from the political system. Now they are speaking of eliminating the "extreme left." Can anyone doubt that their next demand will be to eliminate the whole left, however "moderate" or "patriotic"? Then, in keeping with other historical examples, it will be the turn of the Likud "liberals." Am I being alarmist? Not really. High Court Chief Justice Aharon Barak has just compared Israel's current situation, in the presence of Israel's president, to Nazi Germany. A Holocaust survivor himself, Barak said, "If it could happen in the country of Kant and Beethoven, it can happen everywhere. If

we don't defend democracy, democracy will not defend us!" The Libermans are out to destroy the democracy we have built and create a Fascistan.[2]

A FAKE DEMOCRACY

During the last three years we have seen many signs that the most basic democratic norms are disappearing. Arabs suspected of links with terrorism have had their Israeli citizenship taken away. Arab MKs have been stripped of their parliamentary immunity. Openly racist opinions, political programs and bills—particularly projects for ethnic cleansing of the occupied territories and of Israel itself—have gained legitimacy.

This development could take place quickly, without leading to a major crisis, because Israel has always had an idiosyncratic conception of democracy. Democracy for Israelis has always been restricted to two things: predominance of the majority over the minority by means of elections and the acts of the executive branch being based on laws adopted by a parliamentary majority.[3] This is obviously a rather meager conception of democracy, which completely neglects the concept of rights. Contrary to what has often been claimed, the fact that Israel has never had a constitution is not the sole responsibility of the religious parties. The real reason is that Zionist politicians have never been capable of writing a real democratic constitution, guaranteeing equality of all citizens and fundamental rights independent of the will of the majority. Israel has always been defined not only as a Jewish state (and democratic state, according to the hallowed formula) but also as a country in a state of emergency due to several decades of war. The state of emergency is so deeply rooted in Israeli political culture that neither peace with Egypt nor peace with Jordan nor the joint Declaration of Principles with the Palestinians has been able to put it in question.

We can go deeper into this problem of democracy in Israel. The abrupt passage in 1948 without any transition from Jewish settlement organizations to a state structure made it very hard for Israel to adopt

"norms of governance." Norms of governance are by definition different from the norms that political-military organizations use, which are
not bound by any clearly defined code of laws. (Palestinians know
something about this from their own experience today. They find it
terribly difficult to move on from the way the PLO functioned to the
way the Palestinian Authority should function, as an elected semi-
state that is supposed to adopt democratic norms.) Fifty years after
independence, the behavior of the state of Israel and its political class
still reveals a certain slippage between the state, the ruling parties and
the politicians, and between a binding legal framework and interests
that cannot be contained in that framework. Corruption is one example, of course. But there are also political and military practices that
violate the law but that the executive branch considers necessary,
such as the use of torture and extrajudicial executions.

The State of Israel resorts to two mechanisms to finesse these
contradictions. The first is outright denial, which leads to veritable
schizophrenia. We have witnessed this mechanism at work in the
intelligence services, police, and public prosecutors' systematic lies
about the use of torture; their lies in court ultimately led to a serious institutional crisis and the formation of a national commission
of inquiry. Another example: denying the existence of the Israeli
nuclear arsenal has prevented establishing safeguards. According to
international experts this has resulted in many technical incidents
and made Israeli reactors the most dangerous in the world after
Chernobyl-type reactors.

The second mechanism is the use of personalized legislation.
What happens if the law (in fact a "fundamental law") requires that
candidates for the post of prime minister be members of the Knesset, but Netanyahu, who wants to run, is not in the Knesset?[4] The
fundamental law is amended so that Netanyahu can run. Another
example: a former minister is in jail for corruption, a big campaign
is waged for his release, and a law is adopted allowing certain prisoners to be released after serving half their sentences. Another:

a fundamental law limits the size of the government to seventeen ministers, but Barak, in order to have the broadest possible coalition, has promised cabinet posts to about thirty politicians, and the fundamental law is changed.

Since laws—including laws with a constitutional character—can be changed to satisfy individual interests or the needs of the moment, why not just skip the process of lawmaking altogether? Shaul Mofaz, former head of the army high command, announced his candidacy for the Knesset last year although the "cooling-off period" required by law between his retirement and the elections had not yet expired. Mofaz's argument before the Electoral Commission was almost refreshingly straightforward: if he had been paying attention, changing the law would have been no problem. The only reason the law wasn't changed was pure forgetfulness. So let's pretend it has been and stop wasting time.[5]

The flexibility of laws is one corollary of the absence of a concept of rights in Israeli democracy. Even when rights are mentioned explicitly, as in the fundamental laws adopted during the years of the liberal interval, they are always conditional: "provided that no law exists to the contrary," or "except in case of emergency," or "if this does not contradict the Jewish character of the State of Israel." In short, fundamental rights exist—like the principles of gender equality and equality between citizens of different faiths—unless the parliament has decided democratically, that is, by a simple parliamentary majority, to infringe them.

In Israel, no one has any rights just by being a citizen. Rights— the parliamentary immunity of Arab MKs; the right to run for office if you fail to meet certain political or ideological criteria (which can change whenever the parliamentary majority changes); the legal existence of a party whose program says that the notions of "Jewish state" and "democratic state" are mutually contradictory; the citizenship of Arabs who supposedly have ties with "terrorism," etc.— can be abolished by majority vote. What could be more natural

therefore than MK Avigdor Liberman's party's taking the next step
and proposing in its election platform to strip Israelis who defame
Israel of their nationality, explicitly mentioning rebellious soldiers
and officers, former MK Uri Avnery and lawyer Lea Tsemel?

When a country has created borders that it has continually
expanded in violation of every rule of international law; when the
end, that is, the Jewish state, always justifies the means; then it
should be no surprise that respecting Israel's own rules turns out to
be terribly difficult. Ordinary citizens follow the example of their
leaders, who apply at home the same lack of rules that they have
applied systematically in international relations. The impunity that
Israel enjoys within the international community is not only a denial
of justice to the victims of its permanent aggression; it is also one
reason for the internal degeneration of Israeli society. "But why
should I be the only one in this country who obeys the laws?" the
racquetball player asks on the Haifa beach.[6]

A NEW POLITICAL CLASS

That Israel's political culture and practices have for years borne little resemblance to what is generally understood by democracy does
not make the current degeneration any less real or terrifying. A
recent example illustrates this. Twenty-five years ago Yitzhak Rabin
had to resign as prime minister because of a bank account contain-
ing a few thousand dollars that his wife had opened in Washington
when he was ambassador there. At the time neither Rabin himself
nor the political class nor public opinion considered the young
prime minister a martyr; he had to give up his post as a matter of
course because he had broken the law. Last year, by contrast, a
police investigation implicated Ariel Sharon in a corruption scan-
dal involving several hundreds of millions of dollars. Not only did
Sharon not think for a moment of resigning; backed by the whole
Israeli right, he counterattacked, accusing the public prosecutor's

office and police of being in league with "leftists." He added that the law was inappropriate and needed to be changed.

Another example: five years ago, after a trial that had dragged on for over ten years, the Jerusalem district court sentenced former interior minister and Shas Party leader Arie Deri to four years in jail for corruption. The High Court confirmed the sentence. Hundreds of thousands of people demonstrated for months proclaiming his innocence and demanding that the High Court be dismantled. "Deri Is Innocent" could be read on every wall in Israel and many bumpers. The Knesset voted a special law for his early release. The declarations of Deri's innocence were not based on a different interpretation of the evidence and testimony, but on two nonlegal arguments: "You [the left] condemned him because you hate Shas and Jews of Arab origin [Deri is of Moroccan origin]," and "The rest of them all take bribes, too." Particularly worrying is that a substantial part of the political class, specifically the right and religious parties, joined in the popular campaign against the very legitimacy of the judicial system. During the past ten years the composition of this governing political class has changed completely.[7]

At the heart of this change has been a veritable military coup. Admittedly, the army always played an important political role in Israel, both in its own name and through higher officers recycled as politicians. When Ben Gurion had to resign in the 1950s, he used the army several times, particularly the head of the high command, Moshe Dayan, to force the government's hand. On the eve of the June 1967 war the army forced Prime Minister Levy Eshkol to form the first national unity government, including Menachem Begin and Dayan as defense minister.

Up until Rabin's assassination, however, the high command remained under the government's control and abided by its decisions. The hypothesis has often been put forward in recent years that there is an organized far right current inside the army and various security services, which opposed the Oslo process and took initiatives to sabotage it, including and above all by provoking attacks. This hypothesis has never been proven. But there is no doubt that the army has been the breeding ground for a powerful right-wing current, with General Biran and the successive heads of the high command, Shaul Mofaz and Moshe Yaalon, in the lead. This current has used its power to influence many government decisions.

From 1996 on, the army became a genuine power in its own right in relation to the government. Peres recognized its autonomy, Netanyahu strengthened it, and Barak—his name keeps popping up—made it his true political party. Higher officers sit in on cabinet meetings; military intelligence concocts "information"; the army justifies political and military initiatives and writes the scripts. General Moshe Yaalon was the first to call the Palestinian Authority a terrorist organization, furnished the "evidence," and came up with the scenario deployed from the end of 2000 on to destroy it. Since 1996 higher officers have been making political statements, threatening the government when they consider it insufficiently determined to carry the pacification campaign to its conclusion, and addressing the public directly in order to "explain" the gravity of the situation to them. This has been a true military coup, reminiscent of de Gaulle's 1958 coup inasmuch as it has taken place with the agreement and support of the democratically elected political leadership. It has become an ongoing process through co-optation of higher officers in political party leaderships and at the head of the most important ministries.

But the changed character of the State of Israel's political leadership goes beyond the weight of the army high command. The major role of fundamentalist religious parties on the one hand and Russian parties on the other must also be emphasized. These two political forces represent and give a voice to currents in Israeli society to which references to democracy, the rule of law, and separation of powers and civil liberties mean absolutely nothing. "The composition of the High Court must be changed because it doesn't take account of what public opinion wants," said Orthodox MK Hendel after the judges had declared Azmi Bishara and Ahmad Tibi—together with fascist gang leader Baruch Marzel—eligible to run for the Knesset.[8] A few minutes later a Russian MK expressed his astonishment that this same court had ruled out General Mofaz's candidacy "for purely technical reasons"—that is, because the law explicitly forbade it.[9]

The law of the state does not count for the religious parties; for them only God's law is legitimate. For the Russian parties, democracy and individual freedom are superfluous luxuries and the first cause of what they consider Israel's moral and political weakness.[10] Both currents share a boundless anti-Arab racism. The only difference between them is the Russians' hatred and contempt for believers and religion. This is admittedly no small thing at a time when the religious forces are pushing to install a quasi-theocracy in place of the "Jewish democratic state."

NEW IDEOLOGY FOR A NEW REGIME

Underestimating the weight of these openly undemocratic currents in the Israeli political class would be a serious mistake. Even numerically they already account for more than a fourth of the members of the Knesset and almost half the ministers in the current government. Ideologically the old "Jewish and democratic," non-religious Zionist worldview with its liberal connotations is in full retreat, while a discourse and ideology is taking hold that is reshaping the whole of Israeli culture. The new ideology combines four main elements: a nationalist militarism more or less associated with religious fundamentalism; avowed racism; a die-hard spirit impregnated with messianism; and a willingness to question every democratic norm. Put together, these elements help shape a generalized paranoia, which leads Israelis to view the whole world as an existential threat to Jewish survival in the Middle East or anywhere else.

This new ideology's first and doubtless most perverse effect is acceptance of the domestic state of siege and normalization of death.

Israelis seem to accept the deployment of the army and police on a vast scale and the thousands of security guards at the entrances to all public facilities—restaurants and supermarkets, schools and department stores—without a shadow of a reservation, as if this were a completely normal way of life for individuals and the nation. Sometimes people even seem to accept this state of affairs with pleasure, as if the society finds it easier to live with this reality than with a normality dependent on what the right calls "the risk of peace."

Even worse, the high toll of Israeli civilian and military victims is also seen as something inevitable. The society seems to have gotten used to it with surprising speed, tolerating a government that has proved incapable of ensuring the safety of its own citizens. Nurit Peled, who lost her daughter to an attack in Jerusalem, borrowed the phrase "the kingdom of death" from Dylan Thomas to denounce this perverse adaptation to the death of innocents.[11]

The mixture of aggressive nationalism and victimization produces a level of violence inside Israeli society that can hardly be gauged from outside. But it is enough to listen to broadcasts of Knesset debates to get a sense of it. One MK promises that Arab MKs will face a firing squad; another describes his fellow MKs of the Zionist party Meretz as "traitors." It remains to be seen who will submit the most drastic bill aimed not only at "terrorists" but also at any form of dissent inside Israel. The High Court and the media, but also often the police and public prosecutor's office, are regularly denounced as anti-Jewish or even as a "leftist mafia." Mutual respect, minimal civility and especially commitment to democratic norms are all nonexistent. Democratic norms in particular are viewed as noxious residues of a regime that it is high time to replace with an authoritarian state that will at last be prepared to take the measures required to guarantee Israel's security and Jewish character.

This violence and rejection of the requirements of democracy by Israel's elected officials serve as a model for its citizens. I have already mentioned what the graffiti on the walls and the bumper stickers on the cars say. These attack not only Arabs but also anything perceived as the enemy within, from the "Oslo criminals" that should be brought before a court-martial to the "hostile media," by way of Judge Aharon Barak and the police chief who dared to open an investigation into the Sharon family's possible corruption. The refusal to allow people to stay alive which Israelis express more and more openly when it comes to Arabs —whether residents of the occupied territories or Israeli citizens —is being extended now to Israelis who refuse to howl with the rest of the pack or who would just like to live normal lives in a democratic, secular society. When law gives way to a mixture of clean consciences and force as the basis of relationships with other human beings, then it is sorely missed when freedom needs protecting in one's own community. This is an old truism that Israeli liberals are now learning the hard way.

Violence is manifested not only in Israeli politics but also in everyday interactions at home and in the street. The lack of civility that has always been one of Israeli society's blemishes has mutated into sheer crudeness. While Israelis were noted in the past for their inability to say "please," "excuse me," or "thank you," today they are ready to physically attack someone who cuts ahead of them in traffic; and since they often have guns on them, such incidents sometimes end in tragedy.[12] Psychologists and social workers are continually warning about this escalation of violence, but their warnings seem unlikely to make a difference. The whole society is sick, terribly sick.

THE LEFT GIVES UP

This deterioration of society and its internal norms of behavior worries the moderates in Israel even more than the political situation does. Yet far from gearing up for a counteroffensive, most of the moderates seem to have decided to give up.

During Friday night dinners in middle-class homes the talk is a mixture of lamentation and despair, with a seasoning of paternalist disgust at all the people who are leading "their" country to disaster: meaning Sephardic Jews, Russians, and the Orthodox, not real Israelis like them. These kinds of people found the Kurdish Teddy Bear's interview/confession about his ecstatic bulldozing in Jenin delectable, for example.[13] They forgot about the responsibility of his commanding officers, most of whom were "good Israelis" like them.

First the grandchildren of those whom Tom Segev calls "the first Israelis" were angry with the Palestinians for daring to reject their generous peace offer. Now they are angry with other Israelis for having brought the right and Orthodox to power. As usual, they have no sense of their own responsibility; they just sulk about the ingratitude of their less privileged fellow citizens. The left's demonstrations, against the plundering in the occupied territories and against growing state authoritarianism, have accordingly fizzled out like a burst balloon. The left lost the will to fight a long time ago, in fact as long ago as Rabin's assassination, for the survival of its own vision of society, even for Israel's survival as a nation.

Many on the left are fully aware that the very existence of Israel is at stake. They are sending their children abroad, buying property in Europe, and trying to get hold of a second passport. The Hebrew University of Jerusalem's prestigious mathematics department, which used to be able to boast of its famous mathematicians, has been incapable for over two years now of filling several posts, because even Israeli doctoral students prefer to continue their careers at less prestigious U.S. or European universities.

There was a time when the Zionist left was accused of "shooting and then crying." Today we can say that it bombs and then whimpers in self-pity. Far from fighting for the society that it dreamed of not all that long ago, it is turning inward. It is accusing the whole world, the Palestinians first and foremost, of being responsible for its sorry fate, and dreaming of a more normal future in Europe or the United States. Undoubtedly this will only strengthen the forces of reaction in Israel.

Only a small minority is continuing to fight, both for the rights of the Palestinian people and to stop Israel's transformation into a fundamentalist state that has shed its last democratic pretenses. Will this remnant be able to block Israeli society's rush to destruction, and stop the country from crashing into the wall of hatred around the world that Israelis are building with their own hands? The relationship of forces is not encouraging, and time is short.

Epilogue: Toward Masada?

As all parents know, children learn to recognize their limits during their first years of life, generally by trial and error. But there are children whose parents haven't given them the opportunity for this kind of experience. These are children born with a different destiny, looked at admiringly as they shimmy up the biggest tree in the yard. "This child," they say with a warm smile, "isn't afraid of anything." Sharon is the child who isn't afraid of anything. He's the one who was sent to erase the border during the reprisals, who crossed the [Suez] Canal during the Yom Kippur war, who abolished the frontiers of the Palestinian Authority....[1] Sharon's Achilles' heel is the border that he has never internalized, the spatial expression of his moral universe. Sharon is the only person in the history of the state of Israel who was forbidden to be minister of defense after he pushed back the frontiers of the reprisals that he was allowed to carry out in Lebanon as far as Beirut.[2] The man who refuses to build a barrier[3] will not set any boundary for the son who wants to get rich quick, or the other son who recruited to Likud all the low-life neighborhoods of Ramat Gan and the headquarters of the South Lebanon Army.[4] There has never been an ambiguity this big in Israel in the boundary separating government from family.

The man without boundaries has changed our country.[5]

—ARIE CASPI, *Haaretz*, January 17, 2003

This portrait of the Israeli prime minister is in fact a description of the political class now in power and, to a large extent, of Israeli society as a whole. This society no longer recognizes any boundary, geographical or moral. Its brakes no longer seem to work, at a moment when the Jewish state is skidding down an extremely steep, slippery slope. What lies at the bottom of it? An armed conflict, even a nuclear war, with the whole Arab and Islamic world. Israel's course is unquestionably suicidal, as in the parable of Samson who was prepared to die with the Philistines. This parable recurs regularly in conversations in Israel, each time someone asks what will be the ultimate outcome of this vicious circle of violence, retaliation, and more violence.

Seymour Hersh, the Pulitzer Prize–winning U.S. journalist, calls the Israeli nuclear program "the Samson option." He writes that several Israeli leaders, including David Ben Gurion and Ernest David Bergmann—a little-known scientist who was the father of the Israeli bomb—were determined from the time the state was founded that no enemy would perpetrate another Holocaust. Just as Samson knocked down the pillars of the Philistine house and killed himself along with his enemies, Israel is ready to destroy itself together with those who aim to destroy it.[6] The next war in the Middle East risks being a nuclear war.

The Israeli nuclear option has another code name as well: Operation Masada. The name evokes the episode in Jewish history during the period of Roman rule when the combatants chose to kill themselves together with their wives and children rather than surrender. Identification with the deadly symbol of Masada goes back to the first days of the state of Israel. Only during the "years of normalization" from 1982 to 1996 did intellectuals and scholars denounce both the historical interpretation and the ideological abuse of this episode. Events are unfolding almost as if the Jewish state's tragic end was inscribed in its genetic code in the Israeli collective unconscious; as if in its heart Israeli society never really believed in its own project. Yet it is no longer merely a project. The lives of more than five million Jews, most of whom were born in Israel and the overwhelming majority of whom have no other country to flee to, are at stake.

Israel's degeneration is not just a matter of its extreme militarization and the nationalist messianism that dominate its current political climate. As we have seen, it consists as well in the putrefaction of everything that distinguishes a civilized society from a gang of hoodlums: laws, democratic norms, universal rights and rules. Israel's problem is not so much the Sharon family's corruption or the hold the mafia has on part of the political class, as the legitimacy of these phenomena in the eyes of a large part of its population. Israel's problem is not so much the weight of the religious parties and their ideology in the state apparatus, as the lack of a genuinely secular, democratic movement. The problem is not so much the dramatic rise in violence inside the country as the resignation of those who are in line to be its next victims.

In a sense Israel's mad rush toward its own destruction is taking place as much inside its own society as in its relations with its Arab environment. The country's internal putrefaction could do it in even before the prospect of a total war with the Arab-Islamic world arises. By signing up for the project of a Western crusade against the Islamic world, Israel is opting for a domestic culture war that could in the near future seal the hegemony of a militarist, religious fundamentalism that is prepared to launch a messianic jihad in the name of the Jewish God—and Christian civilization! This is the essence of the perverse alliance between Jewish messianic nationalists and the Protestant fundamentalists around George W. Bush, whose theology, incidentally, is anti-Semitic.

The full significance for Israel of September 11, 2001, derives from this alliance. One of the most effective restraints on Israeli foreign policy has always been the existence of a certain tension between the ultimate, maximalist objectives of Zionism and the interests of the great powers. Even the United States, the most faithful of Israel's strategic allies, had until recently an interest in moderating Israel's expansionist military aims. Regional stability demanded it. But September 11 changed the ground rules, and Ariel Sharon was one of first to grasp this.

For Dick Cheney, Condoleezza Rice, and Donald Rumsfeld, stability is no longer a goal in itself, and certainly not sufficient reason to restrain their own or their allies' military adventures. They are ready to strike out at anything that moves, of course, after having stuck the label "terrorist" on it.[7] Sharon understood that de-legitimizing Arafat would be enough to get him a green light from Washington for a total war against the Palestinians, baptized "eradication of terrorism." The current inhabitants of the White House and Pentagon see Sharon's war against the Palestinian people (and tomorrow against the Arab peoples as a whole?) as the spearhead of the crusade of Good against Evil. If this means that the Jews have to lose some teeth or a limb or two in the struggle, then this is only a down payment on their debt for killing Christ.

Benjamin Netanyahu's intellectual poverty and Sharon's cultural provincialism blind them to reality. They imagine they can use the United States for their colonial project, but they are only a tool for a much more ambitious project, whose goal will among other things cost the Israeli people dearly.[8] As in the age of the prophet Jeremiah, the Israelites' leaders have chosen the wrong side and made a suicidal choice.

Their choice also risks dragging down a big part of Jewish communities around the world into the maelstrom. Israel's behavior on the international scene is making the Jewish state hateful to people around the world, even if we forget the pretexts it is handing to anti-Semites of every stripe. Almost sixty years after the collapse of Nazism, the anti-Semites are beginning to say out loud what they have never stopped thinking but could not say while the survivors were still alive. North American and European Jewish community leaders' unconditional identification with Israel risks being fatal for the communities they claim to represent. They too would do well to reread the Book of Isaiah and reflect on the parable of the broken reed.[9]

True, the new leaders of Jewish institutions in the United States and Europe do not distinguish themselves by their knowledge of the texts that shaped the culture of their forefathers. The often self-proclaimed spokespeople for Jewish communities around the world will also bear their share of responsibility for the looming catastrophe. Instead of drawing on their experience accumulated through centuries of life in the Diaspora in order to warn the young Jewish state, they are fascinated by force, by the image of a Jewish paratrooper who can be as brutal as a U.S. marine. They rejoice at seeing Jews who for once are not denied their rights but rather have the opportunity at last to live their lives without bothering about anybody else's rights.

So is the catastrophe unavoidable? Not at all. Israeli dissidents, marginalized but more determined than ever, are gambling that it can be averted. They know that by defending rights—the Palestinians' rights to begin with, but also rights in general as the foundation of the society they live in—they are fighting to save their own existence as citizens. Israeli society is rushing headlong into a wall. Women in Black, the activists of the Israeli Women's Coalition for Peace, Gush Shalom, and Taayush, human rights organizations, and last but not least soldiers and officers who are refusing to serve are struggling to prevent this suicide.

We are fighting against the occupation, resisting policies based on force, trying to block the fearful prospects of ethnic cleansing and total war against the Arab-Islamic world. But we are also fighting against the philosophy of separation that is confining Israel in a new ghetto, armed to the teeth but more and more isolated. We are keeping the attic windows open to cooperation and solidarity, so as to avoid the other side's giving up for good on the possibility of coexistence. It is an act of resistance—some would say an act of

love—to try to derail this society as it hurtles toward its ow
destruction. The Israelis among us who refuse to collaborate an
the citizens of the world among us must do everything possible and
impossible to put an end to the impunity that only encourages this
country's mad rush toward Masada. Will we succeed? Nothing is
less certain. But this is the only possible way: to gamble on life.

Afterword to the English Translation

On several occasions since the publication of *A Tombeau Ouvert*, even though I was abroad, I wondered whether I had gone too far in my description of the madness besetting Israeli society. I wondered whether my analysis had been too one-sided, too influenced by the mixture of rage, shame, and impotence that torments the members of the Israeli anti-colonialist movement.

But every time I return to Israel, read the week's newspapers, and hear the news reports on the radio, I realize, alas, that I had not distorted the reality and that were I to rewrite this book any changes would certainly not make it more moderate.

Avraham Burg wrote in *Le Monde*: "Zionism is dead, and its killers sit at the cabinet table in Jerusalem. They let pass no opportunity to wipe out everything that had been beautiful in our national rebirth. The Zionist revolution rested on two pillars: the thirst for justice and a governing team devoted to civic morality. Both have disappeared. The Israelite nation is today is no longer anything but a shapeless mass of corruption, of oppression, and of injustice. The end of the Zionist adventure is already knocking at our door. Yes, it has become probable that ours will be the last Zionist generation. There will remain a Jewish State—an unrecognizable, detestable State. After our two thousand years of fighting for survival, our reality is a colonialist state under the yoke of a corrupt clique, a state that makes a mockery of legality and of civic morality. A state run in contempt of justice loses the strength to survive. The countdown for Israeli society is underway."

We may or may not share Avraham Burg's conception of Zionism. But what cannot be denied is that a central figure in the Zionist movement, the former president of the Israeli parliament, former head of the Jewish Agency, son of the historical leader of the National Religious Party and Cabinet Minister Yossef Burg, has come to conclusions that only serve to reinforce the thesis of this essay.

No, there is nothing exaggerated or exaggeratedly pessimistic in this book. All you need to convince yourself of this is to open the newspapers for this week of April 19–25, 2004, an ordinary week. Here are a few news items:

— David Ben Chetrit, an Israeli film-maker, was gravely wounded by four guards stationed outside the Defense Ministry, where he had come for an appoinment with the spokesman for the army. They thought him to be a Palestinian suicide-bomber. His left leg was beaten to a pulp and doctors fear that he will never regain its use.

— Mordechai Vaanunu, the former nuclear technician, was released from prison after serving the entire eighteen-year term to which he had been sentenced for having published information about the Israeli nuclear arsenal. On the morrow of his release the daily Maariv published its own poll in which passersby were asked to choose between these alternatives: keep Vaanunu in prison; expel him from the country; or kill him.

— Abdel Aziz Rantissi, the leader of Hamas, as well as four people in his car, was assassinated with an Israeli missile; a few weeks earlier it had been his predecessor, Sheik Ahmad Yassin, a spiritual authority for millions of Muslims, who was assassinated.

— A majority of Israelis consider nuclear weapons to be indispensable for the security of Israel. According to the polls, the judgment-day weapon should, if necessary, be used to blow up the entire region, obviously including Israel.

— The wall inside the occupied territories was being built at a rate even
   faster than the schedule published by the Defense Ministry. These are
   scenes of everyday Israeli madness. They confirm and underline
   the currency of every chapter in this book.

George W. Bush's permanent, global, preventive war extended a
sort of international legitimacy to the insane brutality of the State of
Israel. Everything now proceeds as if every one of the symptoms
described in *A Tombeau Ouvert* has been incorporated into the new
international strategy: from the targeted assassinations to those
zones of administrative lawlessness, the Israeli detention camps and
their U.S. counterparts in Cuba, Iraq, and elsewhere; abolition of
international law as it had been established after the defeat of fas-
cism, neutering of international organizations, the UN in particular;
unilateralism and preventive war against an enemy that has been
dehumanized and defined by its culture or religious belief.

It is obviously not that Sharon is giving orders to George W.
Bush as some Arab ideologists wrongly claim, nor that Israeli
strategists have penetrated the American administration, nor that
the US government is unwillingly swayed by the effectiveness of a
so-called Zionist lobby in

Washington. The reason why Bush's total war is so much like that
of Barak and Sharon is that both have been grown in neoconservative,
racist, and unilateralist think tanks. There, Israelis and Americans
have for the past fifteen years been strategizing that New World Order,
which is in reality the global disorder of the new American empire.

That Israel went forward in advance of US policy, serving by its
misdeeds as a total-war laboratory for the Bush administration, is
due to the neoconservative team having come to power there several years before their American partners took over in Washington. It
is the Israelis who tested out the neoconservative strategy with its
principles of elimination of international regulation, unilateralism,
and permanent menace of preventive war.

It is in this sense that exposure is useful not only of the Israeli pacification policy against the Palestinians but also of its perverting effect on Israeli society itself, not only to understand the prototypical Israeli-Palestinian situation but also to analyze the course of events at the global level. For with the current policies being carried on by the Bush administration it is the whole planet that is driving at breakneck speed toward catastrophe.

Notes

PREAMBLE: BEACH STORIES

1   Michel Warschawski, *Sur la Frontière* (Paris: Éditions Stock, 2002).

CHAPTER 1: GREEN LIGHT FOR A MASSACRE

1   The "purity of our weapons"—*Tohar ha-Neshek* in Hebrew—
    is the hallowed expression used to refer to the "clean," moral use
    of weapons by the Israeli armed forces.

2   *Hakazat Dam* in Hebrew.

3   B'tselem, "Trigger Happy—Unjustified Gunfire and the IDF's Open-Fire
    Regulations during the al-Aqsa Intifada—Summary," March 2002, http://www.
    btselem.org/English/Publications/Summaries/Trigger_Happy_2002.asp.

4   Amnesty International, *Broken Lives: A Year of Intifada*, November 2001, p. 34.

5   Ibid.

6   The soldiers' destruction of computers and particularly their systematic
    firing on ambulances will be analyzed in the following chapter.

7   A *massacre* is defined in the *Oxford English Dictionary* as the "unnecessary
    indiscriminate killing of human beings." The appropriateness of using
    the concept "massacre" to describe what happened in Jenin is discussed in
    the autumn 2002 issue of the *Revue d'Études Palestiniennes* as well as in
    Tanya Reinhart, "Jénine—la guerre de propagande," in Michel Warshawski
    and Michèle Sibony eds., *À contre-chœur* (Paris: Textuel, 2003).

8   "Retour à Jénine," report excerpts by the 25th mission of the CCIPPP, in *April
    à Jénine,* ed. Nahla Chahal and Hala Kodmani (Paris: La Découverte, 2002).

9   Human Rights Watch, "Summary," in *Jenin: IDF Military Operations*, May 2002.

10 *The Independent,* April 21, 2002.

11 *Haaretz,* April 12, 2002.

12 Article 27 of the fourth Geneva convention (1949) and article 43 of the protocol to the Hague convention on the law of land warfare (1907).

CHAPTER 2: A DOUBLE DEHUMANIZATION

1   "Lockdown" in Hebrew is *seger*; "encirclement" is *keter.*

2   B'tselem, "Wounded in the Field: Impeding Medical Treatment and Firing at Ambulances by IDF Soldiers in the Occupied Territories," Information Sheet, March 2002.

3   International Committee of the Red Cross, "Israel and the Occupied and Autonomous Territories: ICRC Appeals for Protection of Medical Staff," Press Release 02/19, March 8, 2002; *Haaretz,* March 10, 2002.

4   Human Rights Watch, "Israel, the Occupied West Bank and Gaza Strip, and the Palestinian Authority Territories: Jenin: IDF Military Operations," *Human Rights Watch Report* 14, no. 3 (May 2002): 17.

5   The army has repeated this accusation many times, particularly in its response to the complaint made to the Israeli High Court by the Israeli organization Doctors for Human Rights: "This is not the first time that Palestinians have used ambulances in their fight against the army, transporting armed combatants, helping militants being searched for to escape, smuggling explosives, etc." (response from public prosecutor's office to appeal CS 2117/02). Although Israeli, Palestinian, and international humanitarian organizations have repeatedly asked for evidence, the army has never been able to cite even a single case that backs up this accusation. The only time it tried, B'tselem succeeded in proving that the "terrorist" was in fact a doctor, who was released shortly afterward. See B'tselem, "Wounded in the Field," and "Illusions of Restraint: Human Rights Violations During the Events in the Occupied Territories, September 29–December 2, 2000," December 2000.

6   Human Rights Watch, "Israel, the Occupied West Bank and Gaza Strip, and the Palestinian Authority Territories," 29–30.

7   Report by the organization A-Dameer, cited in *Between the Lines,* December 2002.

8   Z. Yeheskieli, "I made them a stadium in the middle of the camp,"
     Yedioth Aharonot, May 31, 2002.

9   Nissim is of Kurdish Jewish origin.

INTERLUDE: THE WALLS' TURN TO SPEAK

1   For several months now the country has been covered with posters
     calling for "transfer," the Hebrew euphemism for ethnic cleansing.
     Radical-left organizations have been systematically covering over posters
     and graffiti calling for killing or deporting Arabs.

2   In general you see general slogans about peace on the same cars
     with anti-orthodox slogans or slogans raising ecological issues.

3   You see stickers calling for national unity particularly alongside leftist
     slogans, less often alongside right-wing slogans. But you see pro-army
     slogans alongside them all.

4   Religious and far-right stickers are often side by side.

5   The followers of Rabbi Menachem Mendel Schneerson (head of the influen-
     tial Lubavitch sect) consider him the messiah. He died about ten years ago.

CHAPTER 3: THE NEW FACE OF RACISM

1   Ariel Sharon's testimony to the U.S. Senate Committee on Foreign Relations,
     cited in Robert Novak, *Washington Post,* June 17, 2002.

2   Ari Shavit, "Sharon Is Still Sharon," *Haaretz* weekly supplement,
     April 12, 2001.

3   Alternative Information Center, *Reports on Settler Violence,* 2001–2002.
     See also B'tselem, *Tacit Consent: Israeli Law Enforcement on Settlers
     in the Occupied Territories,* March 2001.

4   Alternative Information Center, *The Palestinian Olive Harvest,
     October–November 2002, and the Settlers' Violence,* November 2002.

5   1 Kings 21:19 (King James Version).

6   The OAS (Secret Army Organization) was an underground, extremist group
     inside the French army during the Algerian war of independence of 1954-62
     that briefly threatened to overthrow the French government.—Trans.

7   Meron Benvenisti, "The Worst-Case Scenario," *Haaretz,* August 22, 2002.

8   *Haaretz,* December 3, 2002.

9   B. Michael, "Be a Shadow to the Nations," *Yediot Aharonot,* April 22, 2002.

10 B. Michael, "From Tattooed to Tattooer," *Yediot Aharonot,* March 15, 2002.

11 Cited by Amir Oren, *Haaretz,* January 25, 2001.

12 Leader of the far right, anti-Semitic and anti-Arab French National Front.—Trans.

CHAPTER 4: THE WALL

1   See Théo Klein, *Manifeste d'un Juif Libre,* Paris, 2002.

2   Sara Leibovitz-Darr, "Our Fortress Is Closed," *Haaretz* weekly supplement, December 13, 2002.

3   Ibid.

4   Ibid.

5   Verdict of Judge Moshe Drori, Jerusalem District Court (administrative appeals), August 21, 2002.

6   Protocol of the provisional judgment of the Jerusalem District Court (administrative appeals), August 20, 2002.

7   *New York Review of Books,* June 13, 2002.

8   The far right rejects initiatives that prepare for a partition of the Land of Israel.

9   "Fence" in Hebrew is *gader,* which rhymes with "transfer."

10 Nancy Hawker and Sergio Yahni, "Separation," *News from Within,* October 2002.

11 *Yediot Aharonot,* October 2000.

12 Information published by the Israeli Ministry of Defense.

13 Alternative Information Center, preliminary report on the separation wall, August 2002.

14 Information published by the Israeli Ministry of Defense.

15 Report of the PLO department in charge of negotiations— Jerusalem Task Force, August 2002.

16 Vladimir Zeev Jabotinsky was the leader and chief ideologue of the Zionist right during the 1920s and 1930s. His article "The Iron Wall" (1923; published as Appendix 1 to Lenni Brenner, *The Iron Wall: Zionist Revisionism from Jabotinsky to Shamir* [London: Zed Books, 1984]) is the most famous of his political writings.

17 Menachem Klein, "Behind the Iron Wall," *Haaretz,* December 10, 2002.

CHAPTER 5: COUNTER-REFORMATION

1 Michel Warschawski, "Ariel Sharon," *Télérama,* September 2002.

2 Ibid.

3 Arab citizens of Israel are generally called "Israeli Arabs." More correctly, they are "Palestinian citizens of Israel."

4 The Triangle is an Arab-majority area of Israel in the middle of the country, near the line dividing Israel from the West Bank.

5 See the testimony before Judge Orr's National Commission of Inquiry and the reports of the human rights organization Adala.

6 *Praot* in Hebrew, used in literature and history books to refer to Russian pogroms, the 1929 massacre of Jews in Hebron in 1929— and the 1936–39 Arab revolt.

7 *Kol Hair,* December 1, 2002.

8 Amendment 35 to the fundamental law on the Knesset; amendment 12 to the law on political parties; amendment 46 to the electoral law.

9 Bill on "allocation of land for Jewish settlement," 2001.

10 Law on the emergency economic program, 2002.

11 Government decree 1813, May 12, 2002; decree of mister of the interior, May 5, 2002.

12 "Before succumbing to apartheid," statement by the National Democratic Assembly, August 2002; Hebrew translation published in *Mitsad Sheini,* October 2002, pp. 34–35.

13 The "new historians" are a current that, beginning in the 1980s on the basis of archives that were finally made accessible, put in question the old Israeli myths that had denied the existence of Palestinian refugees and prettified the country's history.

14 Teddy Katz had received an honorable mention for his thesis, which proved that there had been a massacre in the village of Tantura in 1948. The veterans of the Alexandroni Brigade, involved in the massacre, took Katz to court. Despite the apparently certain prospect of a verdict in his favor, Katz, sick and under unimaginable pressure, agreed to sign a statement in which he acknowledged that his thesis was unfounded. Although he retracted the statement the following day, this did not stop

Haifa University from rejecting Katz's thesis and terminating his
appointment. Ilan Pappe had not been Katz's thesis supervisor, but he was
the only one who reread the whole thesis and the sources cited in it.
Pappe came to the conclusion that the thesis proved beyond a shadow
of a doubt that the Tantura massacre had in fact taken place.

15 *Le Monde,* May 10, 2002.

16 Ehud Yaari was "Arab affairs correspondent" for Channel 1 for twenty years,
and has now been an analyst for Channel 2 for five years.

17 See the chapter "Les Médias" in Michel Warshawski and Michèle Sibony,
À contre-chœur (Paris: Textuel, 2003).

18 See the interview with attorney Lea Tsemel in the weekly *Kolbo,*
September 13, 2002.

19 See Amir Oren, "The Political Arm of Organized Crime," *Haaretz,*
December 17, 2002.

INTERLUDE: CHRISTMAS IN BETHLEHEM

1   For Meron Benvenisti and much of the Israeli left, Israel should identify with
Western culture; degeneration is equated with the "Orientalization" of society.

CHAPTER 6:

1   "Arafat's Palestine must be destroyed," paraphrasing the Roman senator
Cato's declaration "Carthage must be destroyed."—Trans.

2   *Haaretz* weekly supplement, "No left turn—left-wing intellectuals face the
ideological crisis of the peace camp," October 20, 2000.

3   See Benny Morris, "Peace? No Chance," *The Guardian,* February 21, 2002.

4   Shimon Peres, *The New Middle East* (New York: Henry Holt, 1993).

5   Israel made an explicit commitment in the Declaration of Principles to allow
Palestinians to return who had left (or been forced to leave) the occupied
territories during the 1967 war and the years of Israeli occupation.

6   See Alternative Information Center, "Who will hold the keys to the
borders?," November 1993.

7   Remarks at a conference organized by Gush Shalom, Tel Aviv, September 2000.

8   See Amira Hass, *Boire la mer à Gaza* (Paris: La Fabrique, 2001).

CHAPTER 7: END OF AN INTERVAL

1 "Liberalization" in the U.S. sense: that is, a process of "political reforms tending toward democracy and personal freedom for the individual" (*Webster's Deluxe Unabridged Dictionary,* New York: Simon & Schuster, 1983, p. 1042).

2 The security services were in the habit of arresting Israeli Communist Party leaders, and the marshals of the Labor-dominated trade union federation Histadrut were in the habit of breaking up rallies held by opponents of the Labor government.

3 In 1975 Rabin had called emigrants "a bunch of zeroes."

4 High Court verdict banning torture (1999); High Court verdict in the Kaadan case, authorizing an Arab to reside in a village built on "national" land.

5 Often called "Sephardim" in other countries.

6 Poll published in the daily *Yediot Aharonot,* 1998.

7 Journalist Nahum Barnea has described the Yihya Ayash affair in detail in the newspaper *Yediot Aharonot.* He confirms that the security services had warned Peres that Hamas would respond with extreme violence to the killing of the man called "the engineer." Barnea adds that Rabin had always been opposed to the operation for just this reason. But, unlike Rabin, Peres did not have the nerve to oppose security service officers who wanted "the engineer" dead.

8 On April 18, 1996, the Israeli army shelled a UN base in Kana, Lebanon, killing at least 91 civilians who had taken refuge there.—Trans.

9 French President Charles de Gaulle earned the hatred of the French far right, risking an attempted coup and even civil war, when he decided to accept Algerian independence in 1962.—Trans.

10 Barak had called the settlers "my beloved brothers."

INTERLUDE: END OF AN ERA

1 Extreme-right leader Meir Kahane was the first to call for expelling Arabs and establishment of a theocratic state. "Kahane was right" is his followers' slogan.

2 The Central Electoral Commission is made up of representatives of political parties but chaired by a High Court judge. In 2003, for the first time, the commission took decisions against its chairperson's advice when it

accepted the Knesset candidacy of notorious racist Baruch Marzel and disqualified two Arab MKs, Azmi Bishara and Ahmad Tibi. Later in January 2003 the High Court overturned the disqualification of Bishara and Tibi, while letting Marzel's candidacy stand.

3   Until 1966 Israel's Arab minority lived under martial law, without freedom of movement and denied the most basic rights—except the right to vote.

4   Haim Baram is a well-known journalist, son of ex-minister and Labor Party leader Moshe Baram, and brother of Uzi Baram, former minister of tourism in the Rabin government.

CHAPTER 8: THE NEW ISRAEL

1   Uri Avnery was a combatant in the famous "Samson Foxes" unit in southern Israel, and was seriously injured, during the 1948 war.

2   Gush Shalom website, January 2003.

3   See the survey that the Alternative Information Center held in Jerusalem high schools, *AIC Special Reports,* Winter 1986.

4   For lack of a constitution, the Meretz party managed to push through the adoption of several "fundamental laws," which are to a certain extent laws of a constitutional type.

5   The High Court later threw out Mofaz's candidacy.

6   See the Preamble.

7   Economic power by contrast has so far stayed in the hands of the old ruling classes, which generally vote Labor and live in terror of the fundamentalist, undemocratic populism of the new crop of politicians.

8   Israeli radio broadcast, January 9, 2003.

9   Ibid.

10 See Michel Warschawski, *Le défi binational* (Paris: Textuel, 2000), pp. 97–108.

11 Dylan Thomas, "And death shall have no dominion," from *Twenty-Five Poems* (London: J. M. Dent & Sons, 1936), cited in Nurit Peled-Elhanan, "The Dominion of Death," *Yediot Aharonot,* December 1, 2001.

12 A national campaign called "Thank You, Excuse Me, Please" was organized a few years ago to make Israelis more polite.

13 See chapter 2.

EPILOGUE: TOWARD MASADA?

1   The "reprisals" were military actions that Sharon as head of the notorious
    commando unit 101 led in the early 1950s across Israel's borders, including
    the 1953 Kibiya massacre in the then Jordanian-occupied West Bank.

2   The national commission of inquiry on the 1982 Sabra and Shatila massacres
    recommended that Sharon be dismissed from his office as minister of
    defense. He responded: The people who don't want Sharon as defense
    minister will end up with him as prime minister.

3   Sharon was initially opposed to creating a wall between Israelis and Palestinians.

4   In the Likud primary elections, individuals linked to the Ramat Gan mafia
    and a former militiaman from the Israeli-sponsored South Lebanon Army
    were elected to the Likud electoral list for the Knesset.

5   Arie Caspi, "The Man Without Boundaries," *Haaretz* weekly supplement,
    January 17, 2003.

6   See Seymour M. Hersh, *The Samson Option: Israel's Nuclear Arsenal
    and American Foreign Policy* (New York: Random House, 1991).

7   See Gilbert Achcar, *The Clash of Barbarisms: September 11 and the Making
    of the New World Disorder* (New York: Monthly Review Press, 2002), pp. 92–98.

8   Ibid., pp. 81–85.

9   Isaiah 36:6 (King James Version): "Lo, thou trustest in the staff of this broken
    reed, on Egypt; whereon if a man lean, it will go into his hand, and pierce it:
    so is Pharaoh king of Egypt to all that trust in him."

Index